LONDON BY NIGHT

Frommer's

LONDON
by Night

BY

KATE SEKULES

A BALLIETT & FITZGERALD BOOK

MACMILLAN • USA

a disclaimer

Prices fluctuate in the course of time, and travel information changes under the impact of the varied and volatile factors that influence the travel industry. Neither the author nor the publisher can be held responsible for the experiences of readers while traveling. Readers are invited to write to the publisher with ideas, comments, and suggestions for future editions.

about the author

Native Londoner **Kate Sekules**, author of the *Irreverent Guide to London*, writes about travel, food, and fitness for magazines, including *The New Yorker, Travel and Leisure, Health and Fitness, Time Out,* and *Vogue,* and for the *Condé Nast* Web site *Epicurious.*

Balliett & Fitzgerald, Inc.
Executive editor: Tom Dyja
Managing editor: Duncan Bock
Associate editor: Howard Slatkin
Assistant editor: Maria Fernandez
Editorial assistant: Brooke Holmes

Macmillan Travel art director: Michele Laseau

All maps © Simon & Schuster, Inc.

MACMILLAN TRAVEL
A Simon & Schuster Macmillan Company
1633 Broadway
New York, NY 10019

ISBN 0-02-861210-8
ISSN 1088-4688

special sales

contents

London Orientation

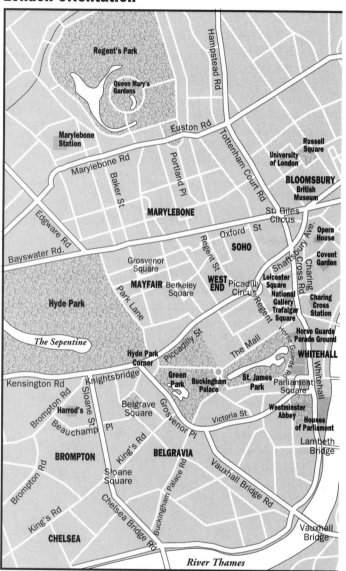

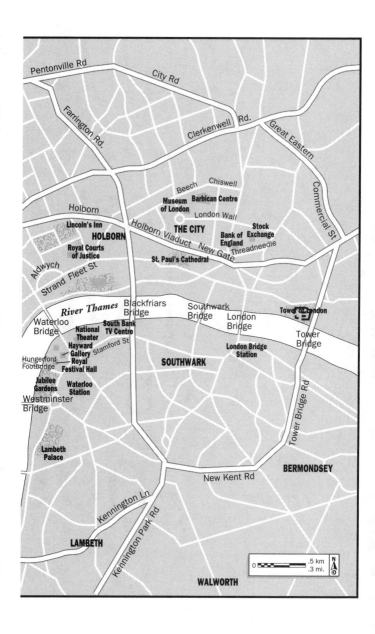

what's
hot,
what's
not

This is a remarkable time for London, and the best ever for Anglophile night owls. London's reputation as a stuffy, unfriendly city that shuts down at 11pm when the beer-marinated patrons of the local boozer stumble onto the wet pavement is out of date. You can also reject the old idea that British food is naught but soggy boiled vegetables, leathery (and occasionally lethal) meat, deep-fried fish and chips, and thin, curling sandwiches. London is now one of the world's restaurant capitals. Even the corner pub serves bruschetta and oysters among the sofas and cappuccino machine. It once was more apt to serve up the local R&B quartet, but pub rock is dying, replaced by a pianist or a jazz trio, which you listen to from your ecclesiastical-chic pew while you tap the bare floorboards that cover a small brewery whose product you're drinking.

What's hot

Bars... More cosmopolitan, more continental than pubs, bars come in more flavors than Baskin-Robbins (which is not the hot ice cream, as it were), and are here to stay. The sweetest genre to come along in years is the **lounging bar**, which is not quite a bar, nor a lounge, nor a club, nor a pub, but something like a public living room—like **The Living Room** in Soho. **The Groucho**, the media/literary membership-only club, has always had lounges, and also has two bars and many imitators, but it's still well worth sucking up to a member so they'll bring you in as a guest. At press time, the **Flamingo Bar** was packing 'em in, as were **The Cow** and **The Westbourne** of Notting Hill—both of those bars being as close to pubs as bars get. Maybe they still are pubs. Often, you can tell if you're in a bar or a pub by looking inside your glass. Are you drinking vodka? You're in a bar. (But you ought to be drinking the happening vodka, which is **real vodka**: frozen shots of aristocratic spirits like the Polish Zytnia, Krolewska, and Zubrówka—with bison grass—and the Russian Stolichnaya Kristal, and Belvedere.) Or is that beer in your tankard? Then you're in a pub. Just make sure it's a **brewpub**. The Orange on the Pimlico/Chelsea border is an independent pioneer; most are Firkin franchises. All are breeding fast.

Further bar tips... Seek out **sidewalk tables**. Just in case there's a summer. And **keep your restaurant table until**

the small hours to possibly circumvent the worst thing about London nightlife: the licensing laws. (See The Bar Scene for more details.) Such laws in **Ireland** are more civilized, but they're about the only Irish thing London hasn't imported. Yes, London's gaga about Gaelic—Guinness, Murphy's, Jameson, and Bushmills, Galway Bay oysters and soda bread; Riverdance (still)— the entire *craic* from the hokey (Waxy O'Connors and other Irish theme bars) to the O.K. (The Fleadh, a Gaelic-tinged festival of music). Raise your glass and say *Slaunche!*

What else is hot in bars... Jazz—always was. Is more than ever. **Smoking**—always was. Is more than ever. Also, from drag queens at Madame Jo Jo's, Ruby's, and the Black Cap to Barbara Cook and George Melly at the Café Royal Green Room, **cabaret** has hit its stride, and is best taken over a cocktail at a small round table.

Clubbing... Everybody's doing it, from teenage to thirty. It's no longer the prerogative of the terminally styled *beau monde* and drug-addled nocturnal *salonistes*, but is for everyone with small clothes and stamina. New things (and there'll be something much newer by now) include **drag kings**—women with chin stubble and attitude. **Multi-use clubbing** is a popular ruse, where multi-roomed clubs adopt variously skilled experts, like tarot readers, manicurists, and hairdressers, and install them somewhere off the dance floor, next to the board games and chill-out rooms. **Goldie** is *the* drum 'n' bass DJ/general music dude, and is doing something fine, whatever it is now, and whichever club he's doing it at. Look out too for that Karma Chameleon, **Boy George**, who's enjoying a second coming as a much-booked DJ.

Sports... Will never vary too much, as long as there's cricket and football. But there's a surge of fascination with **boxing**—all ways, especially women's. **KO Circuit** at All Stars gym is where to learn the ropes. And—not that there are many places to do it—**bowling** is rather in.

Eddie Izzard... There's a name you won't know—because the funniest and surrealest man in England always eschews TV. Despite forgoing the benefits of the audience-pulling medium, this guy's live gigs are always sell-outs. He gained notoriety for his tendency to wear dresses, which he does quite casually, without trumpets. Sometimes he'll do lipstick with a suit, sometimes he'll look like a guy, but his talent's always bigger than his outfit.

Conrans... Love or hate them, **Sir Terence** C's restaurants—Mezzo, Quaglino's, Pont de la Tour etc.—are crowd-pleasers. He started Habitat, went upmarket with the Conran Shops, and is now the ultimate restaurateur, constantly increasing his empire—to the extent that he had to co-found a chef's school to train up enough cooks. One son, **Jasper**, is monsieur le frock, tailor of women's eighties power suits, and still one of the favorites at the shows. The Mezzo waitstaff wear Jasper. **Tom** is a quieter Conran, but one we like, for his own restaurant, The Cow.

Clerkenwell/Farringdon and the East End... These up-and-coming neighborhoods have history and restaurants and shopping and bars and jazz and markets and all-night bagels. **Clerkenwell** and adjacent **Farringdon** were in-between places (between Islington and Holborn, Bloomsbury and the City) until trendy restaurant **St. John** brought to a boil the artists' and bookbinders' and jewelers' studios, the offices of bourgeois left-wing paper *The Guardian*, the first ever foodie pub (The Eagle), the diamond row, Hatton Garden, little Leather Lane market, and various other interesting corners that had been slowly developing. Hop over the City from there, and there's the East End, where New Georgians (like eccentric Denis Sever—see Hanging Out) renovate eighteenth-century Huguenot silk-weavers' houses, Nicholas Hawksmoor's masterpiece Christ Church hosts a June music fest, the Brick Lane Beigel Bake never closes, the Whitechapel Gallery is always worth the detour, and the Sunday morning markets spread enticing tentacles further and further. There's a lot of East End to cover—from Hackney to Stepney—and it's not necessarily easy to penetrate, but keep it in mind.

Culture... is for everybody now. Witness the opera, with sellouts at the ENO and the (temporarily relocating) Royal Opera, and new style divas like **Leslie Garrett** as fresh glamour. Theater thrives, as ever. Physical theater and daring mixed-genre, non-script-led pieces are something to look out for. The incredible pan-Euro **Théâtre de Complicité**, whose *Three Lives of Lucie Cabrol* wowed New York in '96, won't disappoint. There's also an exciting new wave of **female theater directors**, like Deborah Warner, Phyllida Lloyd, and Katie Mitchell. Much arts action is being enhanced by funding from the audiences themselves, via the **National Lottery**, itself a cultural highlight. Where is everyone Saturday evening? At home watching Anthea Turner do the draw.

The Thames... now that dining beside it is better—say, at the People's Palace, the OXO tower, and the Pont de la Tour.

What's Not

Flavored vodkas... Leave the white-Toblerone or boiled-egg (really—at The Edge in Soho) infusions to the kids.

Snottiness... Smile, love, have a heart, and beam happiness around instead.

The Atlantic... The first place in town with a really late alcohol licence velvet-roped its way off the map.

Lloyd Webber musicals... One tune, ten thousand tourists.

Food pubs... So ubiquitous that—although far from unwelcome—we take them for granted.

The Soho House... Latest membership-only club merely takes the overflow after Groucho closes; resembles a singles bar on weekends.

Big, huge restaurants... The intimate salon returns.

Raves... You missed the real thing by several years, but imitations are available at Club UK in Wandsworth, South London.

Repertory cinema... Long-ago closure of the Scala, the Electric, and the rep screens at Camden Parkway and the Renoir reduced the availability of movie-buff houses to a negligible selection.

Tapas... Once trendy, now just something else to eat.

Lunching... The three-martini lunch died with Fleet Street, but the three-hour version had protracted death throes.

Mobile phones and pagers... Like everywhere, for dealers and teens only.

the clu

b scene

As far back as the Roaring Twenties, when the flappers Black-Bottomed and Charlestoned at the Ritz, or whatever it was they did there (actually they did copious amounts of coke), there's been something about London that promotes a creatively festive spirit after dark. The Beatles-Stones-miniskirt-acid-Carnaby Street sixties set the ball rolling, then the Sex Pistols-Clash-bondage trousers-speed-King's Road seventies kept it going, followed by the house-techno-rave-E-warehouse-*aciiiiiiid!* eighties, until now, when all the above, plus the embarrassing in-betweens (nylon flares and disco fever, afros and platforms) continue to come around in ever-decreasing circles.

There are more clubs in London today than ever in history, trying to be all things to all brands of groover. Unfortunately, they and the music therein change four hundred times faster than any book publishing schedule, and since we don't want to look like sad losers, we're reticent about committing to print the sharpest cutting edge of the scene—that's if there is one any more. Clubbing has come out from underground and it's big business. Even bigger businesses sponsor bits of clubs, so you may see Virgin vodka luges, Sony Playstations, Absolut frozen-shot dispensers, free Häagen-Dazs samples, etc., in what you thought was a commercial-free zone.

Where can you still be shocked? Where is the fringe? Well, if you find it, you'll probably feel mighty uncomfortable. The bulk of the clubs, however, are more accessible and less cooler-than-thou since they went mainstream, and since the Soho "Compton" gay scene exploded in the early nineties. As in big U.S. cities, dressing to blur the boundaries of gender is the rule of the night. Unlike in the U.S. (as we go to press), Britpop is big. This is where the Beatles, Bowie, and Madness are ground together, then funneled through a few style-laden, gorgeous boy bands (starring Blur, Oasis, and Pulp) from Camden. The result is either a Spam-like pop product or a worthwhile addition to the nineties music shelves, depending on your outlook. The healthy "indie scene," characterized by nonsuperstar performers, new sounds, and big style, shares roots with Britpop. The number-one fact about clubbing is also the same on both sides of the Atlantic: the DJ rules. Clubs supply dance floor, sound system, lights, and bars, but DJs inject the atmosphere, draw the crowds, orchestrate the action, manipulate the mood, and define clubbing. Some of them work under a banner of an organization (Cream, Club UK, Ministry of Sound, Renaissance). They define clubbing. Usually, a club night is run by such an organization, DJ, or host, and decanted into a particular club for one night per week or fortnight or month. In other words, there's the club as party *night* and the club as party *place*. (We've only put the party places in bold face.) The term "one-nighter" used to cover itinerant parties in borrowed venues, but it's pretty much obsolete now that very little else exists. Even the megaclubs like Ministry of Sound have different flavors on different nights, according to who's in charge of the door and guest lists. You don't need an invite for these clubs, though you'll see flyers for them (the rarest and the best of which have become collectors' items), but you will have to stand in line for them—if they're any good.

R&B, along with Country and Western, is perhaps the only underrepresented musical genre in a town that offers some 400 gigs a week, and in which everyone doing a tour makes a stop. Arena rock usually happens at Wembley, which is a trek and is soulless, so see your U2s and REMs at home. Pubs with music are very London, and there's a vibrant homegrown jazz scene as well as an emergent torch-singer scene in the bars, which is slowly replacing the old-style London pub as the sitting room for the millennium.

Cabaret, the more formal and ambitious version of torch singing, has grown, too, and comedy is as ubiquitous as you'd expect in the home of Monty Python, Ab Fab, etc.

Getting Past the Velvet Rope

Virtually all youth-oriented clubs have a door policy, which varies from "no suits" to "only four hundred of my closest friends get in." Some are stinkingly elitist. If you find yourself in a door pack, look around. Does your age and sexual orientation match? Do your PVC cutoffs and Lurex crochet tank look good around here? Are people's upper lips impersonating Elvis? Don't stand there for an hour not catching the doorman's eye—take the hint, go elsewhere. If you feel bad, know that overcool "no suits here" Soho bar Riki Tik accidentally rejected a besuited Quentin Tarantino at the height of *Pulp Fiction* worship. If you do get in, prepare to be frisked, and/or branded with ultraviolet pen. They're looking for knives and drugs, drugs being a part of club culture that has set off intermittent tabloid hysteria ever since the illegal, Ecstasy-laden warehouse raves of the eighties.

For information, read a specialist magazine—*Mixmag* is good and available at most newsstands. Then trawl the counters at bars and clubwear shops around Soho, Notting Hill, and Camden for a fistful of flyers that give you money off entrance, or invite you in free before (sorry, B4) 11pm. These are planted by the promoter of the nights in question, as opposed to the owner of the club itself. A better class of flyer is handed out as you exit a club or gig. There are also some useful free gay/club scene magazines lying about in Soho—*Prime* is a goodie. Get a copy at the newsstand of the best of the music weeklies, the *NME (New Musical Express),* for an overview of indie and pop, and the monthlies *Q, Straight No Chaser,* and *Wired* for jazz and jazz crossover. For more pointers, *Time Out* is the best source of all-round information, with *ES* magazine, free with Friday's *Evening Standard,* a close second.

Club Rules—What To Wear

London labels: Antoni & Alison, Duffer of St. George, Hysteric Glamour, Stussy, Komodo, Red Or Dead.

Euro labels: Adidas, Blumarine, Fila, D&G.

London shops: Duffer (tel 0171/379–466029; Shorts Gardens, WC2); Bond (tel 0171/437–0079; 10 Newburgh St. W1); Euforia (tel 0181/968–1903; Unit 6, Portobello Green Arcade W10); Ministry of Sound Shop (touristy) (tel 0171/240–5200; 42 Shorts Gardens WC2); Agent Provoca-teur (tel 0171/439–0229; 6 Broadwick St. W1); Red or Dead (tel 0171/379–7571; 33 Neal St. WC2); Vexed Generation (tel 0171/287–3223; 12 Newburgh St. W1); Komodo (tel 0171/379–5225; 35 Monmouth St. WC2); Jones (tel 0171/379–4448; 15 Floral St. WC2).

Bring from home: Carhartt, Liquid Sky, Nikes, Levis.

What To Listen To

Simon Aldridge, A&R supremo who signed Seal, among others, to London label ZTT, explains the terms.

House: Most prevalent form of club music, over 120bpm (beats per minute).

Handbag: Commercial, happy, uplifting, hands in the air, usually with vocal mixes. Named after seventies disco thing whereby girlies dance round a pile of their handbags.

Hardbag, Hardhouse: Harder, faster, darker than handbag, with fewer vocals. (Boys don't carry handbags. Boys are hard.)

Techno: Synth & electronic dance music. 130bpm+. Originated in Detroit, via Kraftwerk. Mostly from Holland and Germany. Complex, percussive, hard.

Garage: Very popular. Deep, soulful, sophisticated people's club music, lots of vocals—divas. Coke scene. Live PAs at big clubs. Also underground—made by kids in projects. Cooler, slinky 110–125bpm.

Trance, Nu Energy: Repetititive, repetitive, repetetetitive, complex, atmospheric, popular in northern UK. From tech-no/ambient, "E" (=ecstasy, the drug) culture. 120–135bpm.

Rave: Old-skool arms-in-air, whistle-in-the-mouth, shirt-round-the-waist, naked torso, Vicks, E in the blood. 125–140+bpm. Some Italian and German stuff gets as fast as a stupid 155bpm.

Hip-Hop: Predominantly black urban American music. Nodding heads, posses, fly girls, one arm raised when a dope tune comes on, whistles. A good hip-hop jam in Hackney or Brixton has the best atmosphere of any club. Drugs, no drinks. Probably ends in a fight.

R&B/Swing: Urban American, tuneful, swing-style beats, commercial mixes. Live acts.

Soul: Older music, dinner and drinks at gig. The classics.

Jungle: Drums 'n' bass. Can't be beaten for apocalyptic atmosphere. Sub-bass, double-time drums. Girls show out (=dance), guys stand around the sides. Best if there's a live vocal by a ragga (=style of rapping that comes from toasting that comes from Jamaica, Studio One style). The most urban, music to date.

Reggae: Dub Jamaican, all vintages, Rastafarian. Has almost entirely migrated from Notting Hill to Brixton.

Trip-Hop: New music form—crossing hip-hop-style beats with ambient soundscapes. Often features low-key rapping, deeply soulful torch singing. From Bristol. Spliff music. Good groove.

Acid Jazz: More live-music-based than trip-hop. This London scene influenced many trip-hop people. Sophisticated. Hallucinogenic, poppy jazz. Jazz Café, Blue Note.

Ambient, Left Field, Ballearic: The off-world colony of club music. **Ambient**—Played in chill-out rooms. Spiritual. Brian Eno invented it. Revitalized careers of Tangerine Dream and Steve Hillage. Mainly Europeans make it now—Dutch, Germans, Italians. Come down to this at home at 5am. **Left Field**—Ambient mixed with techno beats and other stuff. Wide-based soundscapes, from bit of ambient into jungle into techno with movie sound track cut up. **Ballearic**—Anything goes to get you up. From Ibiza in the late eighties, when everyone danced to a lot of different styles of music. Party music, but with serious house undertones. There are still a lot of Ballearic DJs around.

Goa: Named after the beach paradise in South India where shamanic crystal-wielding, occasionally dreadlocked ravers go to spiritually chill. Trancey, ambient, trippy. Hate the term but… New Age.

The Lowdown

The oldies and goodies of dance... Five years is a really long time in clubland; 15 is an eon, so we start the list with an honorable mention for the longest-running one-nighter of all, Gaz's Rockin' Blues, currently housed in the even longer-running (like 30 years), intimate, nice 'n' slightly sleazy West End Swiss restaurant **St. Moritz**. Gaz Mayall (son of near-legendary blues guitarist John) and Rocksteady Eddie spin whole records of blues, ska, and dub for skanking and strolling by all ages, including incognito celebs. Younger by a half decade or so, and the first bringer of Latin, soca, calypso, merengue, and dub joy to town is Dave Hucker's Sol Y Sombra, still going strong, now at **Cuba**. **The Wag** has been at the same location on Wardour Street for-*really*-ever, having been a mod sort of coffee bar/beatnik place in the late fifties, called the Whiskey a-go-go. Now it's in all the guidebooks and therefore hasn't worn too well, but it does keep coming back with a surprise. No surprise needed at the great jazz club **Ronnie Scott's**, but there is one anyway, upstairs: dancing. The night's run by an outfit called Starsky and Hutch as we write, but the seventies thing has surely reached critical mass and will die. Smashing has been the best all-round good-time night for a lo-o-ong time—five years!—during which it's moved about a bit and settled (for now) at **Eve's**. It's long lines and/or friends inside, or forget it. A couple of South London long-players also have long lines: the original funky-Latino-tropical mambistas' *cult*, The Mambo Inn at the **Loughborough Hotel** (no beds), and Up The Junction at **The Grand**, where the *naffest* (Britcool for "embarrassingly unstylish") music and trends from the recent disco past are reborn.

Good for oldies... It's how young you feel, right? But if you're feeling your age, Gaz's has always been O.K., like most anything jazzy and bluesy. Latin and world beat are a close call, now that rhythms other than 122 beats per minute have entered the lexicon of hip, but there's a mixed crowd early on at KISS-FM DJ Gilles Peterson and friends' top funky African-Latin-jazzmatazz night, That's How It Is at **Bar Rumba**, though the median age drops later on. Try its sibling, Salsa Pa'Ti, where the emphasis is also on dance, with lessons to kick off the night. The Mambo Inn at the **Loughborough Hotel** is nondiscriminatory, too. It's best to assume the sixties' and seventies' revival ideas were had by babies born in those decades, and to avoid compulsory navel exposure therein. Something genuinely hippie, and hip again to boot, is the strange concept that is **Whirl-Y-Gig**, a no-alcohol (but BYO), musically mixed (ambient-to-trancey house), all-ages (kid to grandma), balloon-strewn, long-running but early-closing (stroke of midnight) one-night wonder in the east. Over west way in Portobello there's an anomaly in the **Canal Brasserie**, which is a piece of Paris, with its ageless, laid-back groove, good food and pub prices, and waterside terrace. There's not always dancing here, though.

Teenage rampage... There's some leeway re age at the big daddy of big clubs, **Heaven**, because it's usually predominantly gay, in the masculine gender—except for **Megatripolis** night when it goes mixed (=all). **The Arches** is as frill-free as its name, but hosts blasting dance-until-your-ears-dribble nites. Another pair of dance dromes exist in some more arches behind King's Cross station: **The Cross**, which has bits of fairground and garden inside—and hosts the marvelous Ibiza-dreaming hard house Glitterati—and **Bagleys**, which is getting done up as we write, but will no doubt retain its many, many rooms, its podia and plastic palms, its roof garden and its most famous night, Phillip Sallon's eighties reinvention, the Mud Club. At the moment, you have to show your youth ID to get into Camden Town, which is where Madness came from, and which Blur, Pulp, Oasis, et al., now prefer—or so their fans, anxious for a sighting, hope. Actually, pubs are where the Camden scene began and will finish, and the Britpop boys prefer the Groucho (see The Bar Scene). As for Camden's clubs, the **Electric Ballroom** has always been horrible—especially when it was a roller disco—and it's still painted black with fluorescent daubs, but it's cheap, and nobody will sneer at you. In punk days it was *the place,* as was the

Music Machine, which is now the **Camden Palace**. After its redo, it's like a Paul Verhoeven movie, with key lights for all, a bass-blasting sound track, and dance action. Maybe it'll revert to its former studenty image, but it's safe for now. Over at the Lock, where the weekend market sprawls, there's a new lease on life for old **Dingwall's** and its neighbor, **HQs**, where the "Romo" thing was recently happening—nostalgia for the New Romantics, would you believe? Meanwhile, Boy George of that ilk has transmogrified into Mr. Top DJ. Freshman types who bought "Karma Chameleon" as their first disc will like **The Garage**, though Boy has moved on to a hipper scene.

Superclubs... The **Ministry of Sound** heads the list; not that it's the biggest, nor the first, but it's gone the furthest and invested the most in being the club that defines clubbing—the Planet Hollywood of the club scene, with its own shop, record label, and 1995 turnover of some £12 million. Tourists go, but more the Japanese fashion victim than the backwards-baseball-cap type, and with its 1995 redevelopment, it's crammed with virtuality hardware, chill-out psychedelic video games (sponsored), and own-label trance and garage at blood-drawing volume. People like it because other people like it, including top DJs, and that's the secret of its success. Like **Club UK**, **Renaissance**, **Cream**, **F Communications**, **Universe** and other organizations of DJs and club promoters, versions of it clone themselves and appear around the country—and also abroad—and hardcore London clubbers will travel for several hours for one night's partying. **United Kingdom** is Club UK's South London center—an old-fashioned, shirts-off, techno-trance warehouse rave joint. The biggest club by capacity is **Bagleys**, which is usually packed with up-for-it ravers. Two mainly gay clubs that have led the way for about a decade apiece are still giants in the genre: **Heaven** is the aptly named-for-clubbers multichambered, heaving village-under-the-Arches. Brixton's **The Fridge** has room for over 1000, but feels smaller, and has one of the friendliest vibes around.

Lovely little lounges... People rave about (but not in) **Brown's**, which mystifies some of us, since this edge-of-Covent Garden members-only (but you can talk your way in) boîte can be so snooty and dull. The VIP bar upstairs, where you actually do see celeb gossip being created, is the only part worth frequenting. At **The Office**, select from the sweet Wednesday night Double Six Club menu of board games. Antiques, classics, and failures, they're all there: Tumblebug, Ker-Plunk!, Balderdash, and, of course, the great Twister. Things get screechy and heated here, unlike at the **Canal Brasserie** on a club night, especially its Fridays, which are chilled and cheap, calmed by the proximity of water. More canalside dancing is available up north, at the handsome restaurant-club **HQs**, where some nights you should be under 30. **Eve's** is mini, but it's the crowd, the music, the vibe, not the venue, that counts here, so stick to Fridays, for the ever-hip Smashing. Jazz and acid jazz, global beats of many colors, and the occasional hardcore groove meet sofas on parquet floors and flowers on tables at the welcoming, adored **Blue Note**. **Bar Rumba** is also cozy, also roams the world in sounds, and is also a bargain compared to a typical big club's rave night. Jazziest of all is the **Jazz Café**, which is more of a venue than a club. If you take in the gig, you can stay for the dancing, gratis. Best lounge-style clubbing of all is at **Madame Jo Jo's**, where the little round tables and sunken dance floor hosted sexy drag cabaret *years* before cross-dressing went mainstream. Nearby **Riki-Tik**—more of a pre-club bar than a dance club—is lounging for masochists, with its distressed-metal chic and very cool types who look you up and down (see The Bar Scene).

Middle ground... When you don't want to rave or to chill, these are in between. Its name makes it sound enormous, and, to its regulars, it *is* enormous—the two-story **Hanover Grand** is probably London's number-one posing place. Leather couches round the dance floor and a zebra-striped bar are for models, wannabes (of both genders), and model chasers. More fun, more friendliness, and one more floor are at **Iceni**, where the best nights make the most of the three-zone space, with a chilling room, board games, and contrasting DJs. In its time, this Mayfair place has installed hairdressers, masseurs, aerobics classes, you name it. **Astoria** isn't just for gigs, though that's what it's known for. The former theater hosts heaving, hip, hedonistic club nights, mostly for hardcore hipsters.

Hardest... Hardest to get in, hardest beat, hardest to face the dance floor of pros... **Mars** is *it*. It's also hard to get in on certain nights at **Hanover Grand**, **The Cross**, and

Ministry. Hardest to take seriously: **Whirl-Y-Gig** and **Madame Jo Jo's** (also hardest to dislike). Hardest to get home after: **United Kingdom**. Hardest seats and stares: **Riki Tik's**. Hardest to stay still: That's How It Is at **Bar Rumba** and the Mambo Inn at the **Loughborough**.

Something New (Age)... For a long time, Thursday has meant Megatripolis—**Heaven**'s come-one-come-all (mixed, not just gay) night of big sounds, spiritual love vibes, and hawkers of New Age gear in a village of stands around the fringes, and a chill-out chamber called the Telling Cave. Around for longer still, and the most hippy-dippy of the lot is the **Whirl-Y-Gig**, with room for 2,000 (under-12s free), with Monkey Pilot spinning the plates ("Global Ambient Dance," he calls it), with psychedelic rainbow lights and a bit at the end when they toss a vast silk parachute over the dance floor. This scene is going places, with the Back to the Source organization behind many of the best happenings—full-moon parties, tribal Celtic raves, shamanic-ritual sessions, and things we can't yet imagine. It's our tip for the top. Goa—the place in South India, the trance dancing, the sounds—fits in here.

Salsa, mambo, samba, Spanish fly... You've already heard of top nights That's How It Is at **Bar Rumba** and the Mambo Inn at the **Loughborough Hotel**. Both are non-posey, light on attitude, heavy on shoe leather. Both venues host other nights, with a slightly different musical emphasis. Look for El Swing at the Brixton Hall, and the Salsa Pa'Ti in town, both with free dance lessons before. That's a trend that looks set to stick around. At press time, **HQs** had the self-explanatory Salsa Boogie on the Lock, with beginner and intermediate classes, while the West End club called **Salsa** was spinning loads of techno and trip-hop. Just kidding. Try El Mas Latino on Thursdays, and learn by watching the competitors in the Salsa Dance Championships early in the year. **Cuba**, in Kensington, is also for Latin lovers, with its restaurant and bar upstairs and mercifully refashioned dance box in the basement. Sol Y Sombra is the best night. The hippest global groove nights, where Latin rhythms mix it up with reggae/ragga and dub, new and old-skool rap, soca, merengue, and whatever new crossovers have been lately fused, are at the **Blue Note**—which has to have London's most laid-back vibe, without sacrificing its high cool rating—and the **Jazz Café**. Any night with "Mo" or "Magic" in the title will suffice. Amazingly—and near the other end of the cool-o-meter—London has two long-standing flamenco dives, which are more dance showcases, but at the restaurant opposite the North London Forum, **Triñanes**, you can get up and show off your *Bulerìas* moves if you've got them to show. Dance away, but avoid the food. The full-fledged floor show at **Costa Dorada** should be left to the professionals. This place may seem cheesy, but if you hung here every night, you'd see all of London eventually pass by.

Strictly ballroom, soulful, and global... The **Jazz Café** is also one of the few places to find sweet soul music for dancing. Two others are near it in the north: **HQs** (with Soul Circle on Fridays, at press time) and the often-legendary stand-up jam sessions at **WKD Music Café**, where the gay party night, Totally Phunkt, is best for getting down. The classic of R&B, soul, ska, and reggae is Gaz's Rockin Blues, now joined by Friday's Soul Source at the **Grand**—the only place you can bring your Rollerblades. And the only place for many a fringe dance style, not the clubbing type of dance, but just styles that are not being done much, is **Notre Dame Hall**, a big cavern of a ballroom in the West End, featuring Jitterbugs for Lindy Hop to the big-band sound, and Roc La, for the French style of jiving sometimes called *ceroc*—both taught at a pre-party lesson. Line dancing is best done where it came from, but if you're addicted, go to the completely fake tourist theme dive **Big Country**. Finally, a late entry in the nightclub stakes, though it's been there for music and culture for three decades, the **Africa Centre** highlights music from all over that continent.

Boys and boys... The "Compton" scene broke with the decade, cramming Soho with vibrant, new lavender life. Now it's settled in to stay, it seems, though much of it is in bars (see The Bar Scene). **Madame Jo Jo's** has (nearly) always been in Soho, and is now joined by the more underground offshoot drag cabaret club, **Ruby's**, child of Ruby Venezuela, who ran Jo Jo's cabaret for years. Even before Jo Jo's, the **Royal Vauxhall Tavern** had its homey drag cabaret, and it still does. More clubby clubbing is best at the same places where it's been best forever: **Heaven** and **The Fridge**—though pick your night, of course. Queer Nation Sundays at the **Gardening Club** is the chill-out-and-recover-from-the-weekend night, recovering, maybe from the long-running fave Saturday night G.A.Y. at the **Astoria**. Totally Phunkt at **WKD Music Café** is a mellower, soulful groove.

Girls and girls... The latest craze is the drag king thing, which started at Naive, Mondays at **Madame Jo Jo's**. London girls dress to look really authentic as boys. Queer Nation at the **Gardening Club** is for lesbian girls as well as gay guys, but the Girl Bar at **The Box** is only for the chicks, as is the hard house night, Kitty Lips, Fridays at **Mars**.

Members-only hangouts... Sorry, but once you've finished your clubbing years, late-night London happens behind closed doors. You'll be most welcome at any of these clubs—as long as you're the guest of a member. There are overseas memberships to be had, but you have to apply in advance and be nominated and seconded by members. Still, we list them because they are integral to London life, especially the one named after the man who wouldn't join any club which would have him, the **Groucho**. It's stopped being fashionable to knock this place that was started by publishing people and generated drinking stories, gossip, and bad behavior from day one. Get in and you'll see why it's loved—it's smoky, dark, and riddled with squashy sofas, and has a long bar with proper stools (and a newish quiet bar upstairs), a pianist, pretty people, old people, people in compromising positions, and lovely service. Always say yes to dinner, too, since the restaurant's fine. That can't, sadly, be claimed for the **Chelsea Arts Club**, which is otherwise wonderful, with its gardens, dark chambers, and its snooker tables in the bar. It's disreputable by design, but really is often full of pissed sculptors taking their clothes off, having fistfights, or simply falling over, and its annual ball is back on the social map. Accept any invitation to **Brydges Place**, too—a low-profile, older, quietly fashionable West End club, which looks like a comfortable, tall, narrow private house, only with a bar and restaurant, and is impossible to find down a six-inch-wide alley by the Coliseum. A young upstart club is the **Soho House** near the Groucho, which has siphoned off that club's flashiest and youngest members—the ad folk, music-biz types, model bookers, and publicists it didn't want anyway—and since it's open two more hours per night, many Groucho-ists repair there after. **Annabel's** is a surreal mix of early Jackie-Collins-novel discotheque and black-tie supper club. Yes, Fergie, Di, and all the rollicking royals really do drop in on occasion, and a glass of champagne costs twenty quid. **Brown's** is faux elegance for pop stars and their stud-muffins, molls, and hangers-on, and keeps on keeping on as the intermittent place to be for youngsters and old ravers. **Black's** (they do try hard with these names) is the same, only a bit more so, in Soho, with its own restaurant and a menu full of the same old char-grilled this-and-that with arugula and pecorino.

Getting a laugh... England has always had comedy in the blood, and since much of it has gotten to the U.S. via TV, you may be familiar with some of the bigger names. Mind you, the "Whose Line Is It Anyway" crowd (John Sessions, Stephen Fry, Josie Lawrence, Tony Slattery, Paul Merton, etc., etc.) are megastars in their homeland now, so to see them do stand-up you'd be looking at a big ticket item. Many of the "Young Ones" crowd (Rik Mayall, Alexei Sayle, etc.), among others, started at the **Comedy Store**, which is still London's best-known club, and still going strong. Another couple of much-frequented venues are **Jongleurs Camden Lock**, and its older brother, **Jongleurs Battersea**, while the city-border **Comedy Café** has a varied program and something every night. These are drinking-night-out kinds of places, as is the more out-there **Hackney Empire**—a gorgeously blowsy former East End music hall.

Life is a cabaret... Cabaret's many sides, from Barbara Cook to late-night mime, are represented fairly well in London, though there tends to be one of each thing. Cook is often found at the **Café Royal Green Room**, which presents the *ne plus ultra* torch-singer-in-glittery-dress dinner show, and has been undergoing something of a trendy phase lately. Mime is at its most Euro and tough at the **Circus Space Cabaret**, which happens monthly or more often at London's fantastic circus school. For a comic digest of world events, the **Canal Café Theatre** has a weekly Newsrevue, which has proved its worth over years, while at **Brick Lane Music Hall** a simulacrum of a less up-to-date world is staged, with Cockney food. Two of the Conran restaurants do cabaret of sorts. There's usually a jazz trio or pianist, but maybe a crooner, weekends at **Mezzo** and

Quaglino's, and the staircases are glamorous for making an entrance in cocktail wear. Madame Jo Jo's is differently glamorous, and neither Apollonia nor Costa Dorada are glamorous at all, though Damien Hirst, artist-about-town and bad-boy-sheep-killer, did have a Christmas party at the latter, complete with Britpop boys as guests. It's a Spanish restaurant with a word-of-mouth famous flamenco floor show. Nearby, Apollonia does something similar in Greek.

Jazz standards... This week's big name in town will be found at Ronnie Scott's, where cover charge seems less exorbitant since everywhere else has caught up. Reserve a place and bring your gas mask, because London jazz fans still smoke. Pizza Express and Pizza on the Park are in a similar mainstream-but-musically-hip vein to Ronnie's, but serve far better pizza. The latter is very dark—practically candlelit—and therefore more atmospheric, while the former tends to get the bigger names. Meanwhile, there's no food, little atmosphere, but great music (depending who's on, of course) at the Queen Elizabeth Hall and Purcell Room (see The Arts) at the South Bank, where you'll catch the bigger, or more staid folk. Rarities (Hugh Masakela and those Bulgarian choir women, as we write) get to play the biggest South Bank stage—the Royal Festival Hall (see The Arts). Skipping between the famous few and the more obscure, the 606, a basement in Fulham, is a good-time supper club building an ever-longer list of fans.

Different drummers... 606 begins to explore the cutting edge of jazz, but to have this live on a stage, you'll normally have to leave the West End. Go north to the Jazz Café in sunny Camden Town, one of the coolest joints in Europe, or hit Islington's The Rhythmic, which books adventurously and excitingly, and is becoming essential. Northeast a little way, to the city border, Blue Note has great, great gigs, as well as club nights. Further northeast, the Stoke Newington Vortex is the most cutting-edge of all major London jazz venues, musically speaking—which can mean self-conscious whoops during interminable drum solos, or a blast of aural heaven. Crouch End is as far from civilization as it sounds (except to the social-worker and artist locals), but the King's Head has great jazz gigs, especially the weekly appearance of the house band, Changes. Look in the listings for another ton of free or cheap pub gigs, especially on weekends. Higher quality than most, though way out in Barnes, is the riverside **Bulls Head**.

Eight to the bar... R&B, soul, blues, rock and roll—there's more of this live in London than via DJs in clubs. In the West End, the venerable **100 Club** still serves it up—all the above—in the correct smoky room with peeling paint and beer puddles. The cut-rate, West London version of same is the **Bottom Line**, while the Covent Garden **Roadhouse**, when it has a live band, is tourist-themed, Harley-on-the-bar, but fun anyway. The best unknown place for quaint, homegrown rootsy blues is the backwater grungy pub, the **Station Tavern**, while the capital of big names of blues-roots-folk is the **Twelve Bar Club**, which *Time Out* readers voted the best venue in town in 1995. The **Dublin Castle** puts on a good deal of R&B of the homegrown, sometimes amateurish, kind.

Indie bandstands and where to unplug... When Nirvana was an unknown American indie band, it played the **Bull & Gate**, the original dive of an up-and-coming bands' venue, where the stage glowers in a bare, black, nearly seatless hall, that empties out between bands, during bad support acts, and on the wrong night. It's nearly next to the Forum. There's another great pub venue a mile away by the Jazz Café, the one where Madness (who sang Camden into existence) came from, the **Dublin Castle**. Again, it's no-frills, and there are miserable nights interspersed with greats. Another longstanding venue showcasing new bands is the **Rock Garden**, slap in the middle of Covent Garden. It's horrible—a sweaty basement with a mysteriously bad vibe, and an apparently random booking policy. Back north, **The Garage**, one of many tentacles of the Mean Fiddler organization, has two layers: the main room for the artists who've built up a following, and the **Upstairs** acoustic room for a mixture of revivals, obscurities, and bigger acts unplugged. The **Mean Fiddler** itself, which is in godforsaken Harlesden, has its **Acoustic Room**, too, which books interesting acts, while its club sibling, **Subteranea**, gets the hardest, hippest, often non-British, acts, five seconds before they explode into fame.

Top rock... The medium range of performers, not the megastars, and not the underground heroes, play at a

LONDON ⟨ THE CLUB SCENE

selection of reasonably atmospheric halls, which tend—this being the U.K.—to throw you out at 11pm, though you can increasingly get lucky and stay till midnight. Heading the list are two former ballrooms, **The Forum**, in a corner of Kentish Town, and the **Astoria**, in the most central location possible—opposite Centrepoint. Neither is well-off for seating. In the same breath, though a little louder, should be mentioned two former theaters—the **Shepherds Bush Empire** and the Clapham **Grand**. See the listings for a precise idea of how this quartet positions itself in relation to itself. In Brixton, the capacious **Academy** and **The Fridge** also offer live sets by this stratum of medium-to-big star.

Bigger, bigger, biggest... Mainstream, platinum-selling people pack out the Hammersmith **Apollo**. If they have taste and they can possibly fit in, they prefer the nearby **Shepherds Bush Empire**, while the **Royal Albert Hall** (see The Arts) hosts those who aren't even trying to be alternative—including Eric Clapton for his traditional 10 days in February, known as "the Erics." Similarly, the **Royal Festival Hall** and the **Barbican** (see The Arts) sometimes invite popular music artistes onto their stages. The gigantic stars have no choice but to book into **Wembley**, which comes in a selection of flavors, most often the **Arena** and the **Stadium**. Like giant rock stadia anywhere, they're way out of town.

Folkies and Irish rebels... The newish breed of Irish theme-pub, as opposed to seedy Irish dives that have been around since the Middle Ages, usually provide a performer or two, sometimes tongue-in-cheek faux folk, but a nice background for drinking. The over-the-top **Waxy O'Connor's** does this. For the real thing, complete with bad neighborhood, go to Kilburn, and the **National**. All other folk styles, blues to zydeco, visit the Islington **Weavers** eventually, while **The Vine** in the music corner of Kentish Town (with the Bull & Gate, the Forum, and Triñanes on the doorstep) is another predominantly Gaelic showcase. **Cecil Sharp House** is the stately home of London folk music, an elegant Regency House on the fringe of Camden Town, which has a weekly, friendly, extemporary club, and many a special gig, with maybe a dance lesson thrown in.

The Index

Africa Centre. It is indeed a center for African culture, and about the best in all Europe, too, since 1962 (it's possible they haven't redecorated). Events are wide-ranging—gigs, club nights, dance, theater—plus a restaurant, and all in the heart of Covent Garden.... *Tel 0171/836–1973. 38 King St. WC2, Covent Garden tube stop. Open late club nights, otherwise 11pm. Closed Sunday. Cover charge for clubs and music.*

Annabel's. Whatever the opposite of a dive is, this *strictly* members-only Berkeley Square boîte is it. Nobs, snobs, and hoorays (braying, chinless Hooray Henry is the Sloane Ranger's brother) are those members. Surprisingly, it can be a blast.... *Tel 0171/629–3558. 44 Berkeley Square W1, Queen Park tube stop.*

Apollo Hammersmith. The former Hammersmith Odeon used to be a movie theater, and now hosts biggish rock names, with no dancing at the front, please.... *Tel 0171/416–6080. Queen Caroline St. W6, Hammersmith tube stop. Cover charge.*

Apollonia. There's quite a Greek/Cypriot community in London, but this basement restaurant isn't the most authentic of the places it owns here. It is, however, the place to go for a plate-smashing belly-dancing, let-your-hair-down floor show, with kebab.... *Tel 0171/637–3724. 17A Percy St. W1, Tottenham Court Road tube stop. Open till 1am. Offers Sun lunch.*

The Arches. Nostalgia for the rave days, not the WWII air raids that these provided shelter against. About 1,200 kids can squeeze in, for sounds louder than sirens.... *Tel 0171/357–6753. 53 Southwark St. SE1, London Bridge tube stop. Open late. Cover charge.*

Astoria. Very central, at the top of Oxford Street, this big former ballroom on the corner has a pleasantly louche vibe, for wrecks in their twenties to see bands on the up, and some of the best club nights.... *Tel 0171/434–0403. 157 Charing Cross Rd., Tottenham Court Road/Leicester Square tube stop. Late opening. Cover charge.*

Bagleys. Behind King's Cross railway station in a very unsalubrious neighborhood, there are a couple of vast clubs—this one, and the Cross. This one's bigger, and after its refit, snazzier.... *Tel 0171/278–4300. Kings Cross Freight Depot, York Way N1, Kings Cross tube stop. Open till 6am. Closed some days (call). Cover charge.*

Bar Rumba. In the terrible Trocadero pseudomall, steps from Soho and even nearer Eros (the Piccadilly Circus statue), this unpretentious, none-too-splendid-looking club is for Latin lovers. That's How It Is is the king night.... *Tel 0171/ 287–2715. 36 Shaftsbury Ave. W1, Piccadilly Circus tube stop. Open till 6am. Closed some days (call). Cover charge.*

Big Country. This is the only place that understands the Tush Push, though you'll have to put up with roadhouse buffalo wings and possibly a depressingly half-empty hall, since the London cowboy contingent isn't big enough for Big Country. Line dance lessons most days.... *Tel 0171/753–8020. 17–19 Great Windmill St. W1, Covent Garden tube stop. Open till 3:30am. Closed Sun. Cover charge some nights.*

Black's. Soho members-only club for groovers who've made it far enough to afford membership while they're still young enough to pose gorgeously.... *Tel 0171/287–3381. 67 Dean St. W1, Leicester Square tube stop.*

Blue Note. A chill and chic double-decker club on the edge of the city, where sounds center on jazz and global, with some seriously hard nights, too.... *Tel 0171/729–8440. 1 Hoxton Square N1, Old Street tube stop. Open till 6am. Closed some days (call). Cover charge.*

Bottom Line. A dive of a rock hall with more or less mainstream tastes (not the place for indie bands or jungle) for good-time music; lots of blues.... *Tel 0181/749–1114. 58 Shepherds Bush Green W12. Closed some nights (call). Cover charge.*

The Box. A Covent Garden bar that has a well-liked gay girls' night helpfully known as Girl Bar, Sundays.... *Tel 0171/ 240–5828. Monmouth St, Seven Dials, WC2, Leicester Square tube stop. Open till 11pm.*

Brick Lane Music Hall. In what was once a main London brewery, this now re-creates the golden age of music hall— Britain's less risqué burlesque—after serving three courses of unpredictable food (salt beef and latkes? fish and chips? curry?) in the heart of the Cockney East End.... *Tel 0171/ 377–9797. 152 Brick Lane E1. Open till 11pm. Closed some nights (call).*

Brixton Academy. A huge hall in South London's reggae-culture neighborhood tends to be very hip and pretty young, and has bands playing most nights, as well as club events.... *Tel 0171/924–9999. 211 Stockwell Rd. SW9, Brixton tube stop. Late opening. Cover charge.*

Brown's. Members only, but if you're famous and gorgeous, you'll make it upstairs to the VIP bar, which is the bit to be in—a Pamela Anderson–Tommy Lee sort of place (the U.K. *loves* Pammie). There are club nights in the plush surroundings, and a good deal of attitude.... *Tel 0171/831–0802. 4 Great St., Kingsway WC2, Holborn tube stop. Open till 7am. Cover charge.*

Brydges Place. Tall, thin, and patrician, this is the sitting room you'd like to have if you lived here. Members only, though.... *Tel 0171/836–1436. 2 Brydges Place WC2, Charing Cross tube stop.*

Bull and Gate. A tenacious representative of a dying breed: the London pub with a back room for bands. This is the place where upstarts and stars on the up get an early outing, alongside the egregiously awful, and it can be pretty darn hip.... *Tel 0171/485–5358. 389 Kentish Town Rd. NW5, Kentish Town tube stop. Open till 11pm. Cover charge.*

Bull's Head. By the Thames in Barnes, this pretty pub has attracted serious jazz buffs (those with beards who whoop during bass solos) for years and years.... *Tel 0181/876– 5241. Barnes Bridge, Barnes Bridge BR or #9 bus. Cover charge sometimes.*

Café Royal Green Room. Salubrious in extremis, this red-carpet salon serves a sit-down three-course supper (good food, too), while the well-known crooner croons in sequins from the stage, then cheek-to-cheek dancing is done. On other floors are an award-spattered restaurant and a black-tie cocktail bar—all so unfashionable it's become fashionable.... *Tel 0171/437–9090. 68 Regent St. W1, Piccadilly Circus tube stop. Open till 3am. Closed Sun–Mon. Cover charge.*

Camden Palace. A big old club at the foot of this youth borough, where huge sound, lighting, and dancing can be looked down upon from several circles of hell. The Palace was a nerdy place until its recent refurbishing.... *Tel 0171/ 387–0428. 1A Camden High St. NW1, Camden Town tube (Mornington Crescent when it reopens). Open till 8am. Closed some days (call). Cover charge.*

Canal Brasserie. A civilized little boîte down by the waterside, in a rather godforsaken offshoot of Notting Hill/Portobello, this is just a restaurant sometimes, a club at others.... *Tel 0181/960–2732. Canalot Studios, 222 Kensal Rd. W10, Westbourne Park tube stop. Open till 2am. Closed some days (call). Cover charge.*

Canal Café Theatre. Its Little Venice waterside location is a bonus; there's a late cabaret after the play.... *Tel 0171/ 289–6054. Bridge House, Delamere Terrace W2, Warwick Av. tube stop.*

Cecil Sharp House. An elegant house in Camden, but far from the madding Camden teens, this holds folk soirées for hardcore listeners to trad British music and its American brethren (Cajun, zydeco, banjo); sometimes with a dance lesson, too.... *Tel 0171/485–2206. 2 Regents Park Rd. NW1, Camden Town tube stop. Closed some days (call). Cover charge.*

Chelsea Arts Club. Progenitor of the infamous Chelsea Arts Club Ball, wherein artists and artistes pose in small costumes and disgrace themselves, neither club nor ball are as naughty as they once were, though an invitation to penetrate the private white walls is still cause for joy.... *Tel 0171/376–3311. 3 Old Church St. SW3, Sloane Square tube stop.*

Circus Space. London's one and only circus school is in a converted power station, and is really something—full-scale flying rigs and all. Think Cirque du Soleil, not Barnum and Bailey.... *Tel 0171/613–4141. Coronet St. N1, Old Street tube stop. Call for times. Cover charge.*

Comedy Café. A city club with a varied program—and times. Call for the latest.... *Tel 0171/739–5706. 66 Rivington St. EC2, Old Street tube stop. Cover charge some nights.*

Comedy Store. The first—and if not the best, at least one of the most reliable—of funny clubs.... *Tel 01426/914433 (info), 0171/344–4444 (credit card res.). Haymarket House, Oxendon St. SW1, Piccadilly Circus tube stop. Closed Mon. Cover charge.*

Costa Dorada. A restaurant secreted behind the end of Oxford Street, which is really a Spanish fairground, in which every Londoner, hip and famous to nerd, has spent at least one memorable but drunken night. The flamenco shows are better than the average, but food is compulsory; there's a tapas bar, and a Colombian night Sundays.... *Tel 0171/636–7139. 47–55 Hanway St. W1, Tottenham Court Road tube stop. Open till 3am (1am Sun). AE not accepted.*

The Cross. Another place in the King's Cross hinterlands, much more intimate than its huge neighbor, Bagleys, this has a rep for hosting hard DJs, hep kids, and good dance.... *Tel 0171/837–0828. Goods Way Depot, York Way N1, Kings Cross tube stop. Open till 6am. Closed some days (call). Cover charge.*

Cuba. A bar-restaurant upstairs, a club downstairs, this somewhat odd Kensington place attracts a cross section of ages and types who come for the Latin beat, but mainly to drink after hours, especially on nights when the cover is waived.... *Tel 0171/938–4137. 11 Kensington High St. W8, High Street Kensington tube stop. Open till 3am. Cover charge most nights.*

Dingwall's. The big old place in Camden Lock that was rebuilt for a new generation a couple years back.... *Tel 0171/267–1999. Camden Lock NW1, Chalk Farm tube stop.*

Dublin Castle. A Camden pub with bands, but one that brought local boys, Madness, to the masses, and one that continues to supply the odd steaming night out.... *Tel 0171/ 485–1773. 94 Parkway NW1, Camden Town tube stop. Open till 11pm. Cover charge.*

Electric Ballroom. A big club in the epicenter of Camden attracts kids who aren't too near the cutting edge of groove, but who like to party with gusto and large drinks.... *Tel 0171/485–9006. 184 Camden High St. NW1, Camden Town tube stop. Open till 3am. Closed some days (call). Cover charge.*

Eve's. A small West End club that's in here mainly because of its Friday night resident, Smashing—a friendly night, if you already know its crowd.... *Tel 0171/TK. 189 Regent St. W1, Piccadilly Circus tube stop. Open till 3am. Closed some days (call). Cover charge.*

Forum. A well-loved and well-frequented former ballroom in the north hosts medium-famous, medium-hip bands, usually for the twenties set, though older performers do attract older kids.... *Tel 0171/284–2200. 9–17 Highgate Rd. NW5, Kentish Town tube stop. Cover charge.*

The Fridge. One of London's most embracing atmospheres is a mysteriously regular feature of this Brixton big club—which is mainly gay.... *Tel 0171/326–5100. Town Hall Parade SW2, Brixton tube stop. Open till 4am. Closed some days (call). Cover charge.*

Garage. Part club, part music venue, this North London dive will take you half an hour to reach from town, has varied nights, but is usually notably young and grungy.... *Tel 0171/607– 1818. 22 Highbury Corner. Highbury and Islington tube stop. Open till 3am. Cover charge.*

Gardening Club. Usefully central, this place has shaped up into a long-runner, with the Sunday Queer Nation still the place to chill after a hard week's clubbing, gay or straight. There's also a second one, much, much bigger.... *Tel 0171/497– 3154. 4 The Piazza, Covent Garden tube stop. Open late. Cover charge.*

The Grand. In the south of the river adventure zone are a few classic calls for the clubbing kid, and this is one—especially for Up the Junction, which is fun, fun, seventies fun.... *Tel 0181/961–5490. St. Johns Hill SW11, Clapham Junction tube stop. Open till 2am. Closed some days (call). Cover charge.*

Groucho. You can't get in unless you know a member, but this is so integral to the life of the London intelligentsia (drinking division) that it can't be left out.... *Tel 0171/439–4685. 44 Dean St. W1, Leicester Square tube stop.*

Hackney Empire. In the East End is this rejuvenated music hall, looking like an opera house that's fallen on hard times, and staging lots of good events, mainly comedy and cabaret, but also musical numbers.... *Tel 0181/985–2424. 291 Mare St. E8, Hackney Downs tube stop. Cover charge.*

Hanover Grand. At press time, very hip among pretty youth, but by now who knows? It's a West End, two-tier wonderland of swanky décor and heaving dance floor.... *Tel 0171/499–7977. 6 Hanover St. W1, Oxford Circus tube stop. Open till 5am. Cover charge.*

Heaven. A venerable and vast (mostly) gay dance club under the arches behind Charing Cross has the boomingest bass and laser lights—they give you the bends.... *Tel 0171/839–3852. Craven St. WC2, Charing Cross tube stop. Open till 4am. Cover charge.*

HQs. Another Camden destination, this is a rather handsome club with a restaurant, perched above the Lock where the weekend market lives. It's tailored for dedicated dancers in their twenties, but check listings for other sorts of evenings.... *Tel 0171/485–6044. Camden Lock, West Yard NW1, Chalk Farm tube stop. Open till 2am. Closed some days (call). Cover charge.*

Iceni. One of London's favorite multi-room clubs, featuring tarot readers, manicurists, board games, and the famous Flipside Dating Service.... *Tel 0171/495–5333. 11 White Horse St. W1, Queen's Park tube stop. Open till 3am.*

Jazz Café. A converted bank in downtown Camden hosts the hottest combos from all over the place, and consistently swings. It's worth getting tickets in advance and booking a table if you can (they don't always let you).... *Tel 0171/916–6000. 5 Parkway NW1, Camden Town tube stop. Cover charge.*

Jongleurs Battersea. Older brother of the newer Camden one, this is rated very highly by comedy aficionados. Some nights run late.... *Tel 0171/924–2766. The Cornet, 49 Lavender Gardens SW11, Clapham Junction BR. Cover charge.*

Jongleurs Camden Lock. If you like the seething teenage tornado of Camden Lock, you'll laugh at the funny guys here. Actually, most people seem to do so.... *Tel 0171/924–2766. Dingwalls Building, Middle Yard, Camden Lock NW1, Chalk Farm tube stop.*

King's Head. Crouch End is not a neighborhood you come across on your way to anywhere, but if you fancy a real local night out among friendly arty schoolteacher types, this pub's Wednesday regular jazzers, called Changes, are very good.... *Tel 0181/340–1028. 2 Crouch End Hill N8, Finsbury Park tube, and W7 bus. Open till midnight. Cover charge.*

Loughborough Hotel. A little Brixton dive that's remarkable for one thing only: the Mambo Inn, which has spawned a subculture of its own, and is always packed with salsa, lambada, and samba mambistas: a.k.a. dance fans.... *Tel 0171/737–2943. Loughborough Rd. SW9, Brixton tube stop. Open till 3:30am. Mambo Inn Fri–Sat. Cover charge.*

Madame Jo Jo's. The original drag cabaret in central Soho, complete with little round tables, was a great place to go before it opened out into a full-fledged club, and now hosts some of the hottest nights. Naive on Mondays was London's first outing for Drag Kings.... *Tel 0171/734–2473. Brewer St. W1, Piccadilly Circus tube stop. Open till 3am. Closed some days (call). Cover charge.*

Mars. This intimate, rather shabby dive of a club opposite the Astoria is known for being on the cutting edge.... *Tel 0171/439–4655. 12 Sutton Row, W1, Tottenham Court Road tube stop. Open till 6am. Open three nights/week (call). Cover charge.*

Mean Fiddler. The mothership of an operation with its tentacles all over the London live-music scene, this good-time venue is none too central. Bands are not the hottest, but are often the kind with a following that likes to bop.... *Tel 0181/961–5490. 28A High St., Harlesden NW10, Willesden Junction tube stop. Open late. Cover charge.*

Mezzo. A Conran special. The biggest restaurant in Europe, and one of several of Sir Terence's brainchildren in the capital, this has a cabaret stage for a jazz trio, plus dancing on Fridays and Saturdays.... *Tel 0171/314–4000. 100 Wardour St. W1, Bond Street tube stop. Open till 3am (Fri–Sat).*

Ministry of Sound. If you're a clubbing type with only time for one outing, this is one of the biggest and most serious venues in town, with its own merchandizing operation, record label, attitude, clothing, and loads of different areas/ dance floors/chill-out rooms. Most people rate highly the techie décor, cyber props, heavy, heavy sound systems, and the buzz, but the most snotty find it far too commercial to be "the" place.... *Tel 0171/378–6528. 103 Gaunt St. SE1, Elephant & Castle tube stop. Open till 8am. Closed some days (call). Cover charge.*

The National. Kilburn is London's Irish neighborhood, and there's nothing designer about it. For those who crave authenticity, this is the biggest music venue in NW6.... *Tel 0171/328–3141. 234 Kilburn High Rd. NW6, Kilburn tube stop. Cover charge.*

Notre Dame Hall. Bang in the center of town, this ballroom contains a variety of clublike nights, often featuring a particular dance style you can't often do in public, like the French jive or jitterbug. Good atmosphere, and maybe a class to kick off.... *Tel 0171/437–5571. 5 Leicester Place WC2, Leicester Square tube stop. Opening hours and days vary. Cover charge.*

The Office. The décor at this West End place doesn't make too many concessions to clubland, but they're not needed on the Wednesday nights that put it in this book. That's when the Double Six Club is on, with its board games and easy-listening tracks, and funny-ha-ha atmosphere. Reservations advisable.... *Tel 0171/636–1598. 3–5 Rathbone Place W1, Tottenham Court Road tube stop. Open till 3am. Closed some days (call). Cover charge.*

100 Club. A venerable dive that concentrates on rock and jazz, blues, and R&B, with live bands and dance night.... *Tel 0171/636–0933. 100 Oxford St. W1. Oxford Circus tube stop. Cover charge.*

Pizza Express. A big jazz venue, and London's best pizzas, too. This tends to host mainstream performers.... *Tel 0171/ 437–9595. 10 Dean St., Tottenham Court Rd tube stop. Cover charge.*

Pizza on the Park. As above, westerly version.... *Tel 0171/ 235–5273. 11 Knightsbridge SW1, Hyde Park Corner tube stop. Cover charge.*

Quaglino's. This is the older Conran huge glamourous restaurant that has live music (see **Mezzo**). The dancing was discontinued, but the jazz goes on, weekends. See Late Night Dining.

The Rhythmic. This place—the newest of London's major jazz venues—has great talent in the booking department. Irresistible lineups of greats and legends mixed up with local heroes, in the middle of Islington's daytime fruit-and-veg market.... *Tel 0171/713–5859. 89–91 Chapel Market N1, Angel tube stop. Open late. Cover charge.*

The Roadhouse. It's a touristy, theme-y cavern of a Covent Garden bar, but useful when you're around here, and sometimes the band gets a good steam up. They had an indoor Harley here before the Harley franchise.... *Tel 0171/240– 6001. Jubilee Hall, 35 The Piazza WC2, Covent Garden tube stop. Open late. Cover charge some nights.*

Rock Garden. Not so much a recommendation, but more of a listing for this famous Covent Garden dive, which books new bands nobody else will book, and which has club nights that are limp and sweaty.... *Tel 0171/836–4052. 6–7 The Piazza WC2, Covent Garden tube stop. Open late. Cover charge.*

Ronnie Scott's. London's best-known and most-loved jazz venue is going very strong, still run by saxophonist Ronnie, and still hosting the hottest lineups, for which you usually must book. Upstairs at Ronnie's turns into a not-especially-jazzy club venue at least two nights a week.... *Tel 0171/ 439–0747. 47 Frith St., Leicester Square tube stop. Open late. Cover charge.*

Royal Vauxhall Tavern. Just an old South London pub that happens to have hosted drag shows all its life, and still does so.... *Tel 0171/582–0833. 372 Kennington Lane SW8, Vauxhall tube stop. Open late (not Sun).*

Ruby's. Ruby Venezuela split from Madame Jo Jo's to follow her dream—a club of her very own, complete with drag cabaret to rival the glitteriest beauty pageant.... *No telephone. 13 Gerrard St. W1, Leicester Square tube stop. Open till 3am (11pm Sun). Cover charge.*

St. Moritz. A former heavy-metal hole in a Swiss restaurant (really) now has the pleasure of offering one of London's longest-running one-night-a-week clubs, Gaz's Rockin' Blues on Thursdays. It's lasted because its ska and rocksteady, R&B and blues, rock 'n' roll and reggae spun without attitude makes a mixed bag of people happy.... *Tel 0171/437–0525. 159 Wardour St. W1, Tottenham Court Road tube stop. Open till 3.30am. Closed some days (call). Cover charge.*

Salsa. As a restaurant, this is a great Latin club, with dance lessons early on most evenings, and sounds from Brazil, Colombia, Mexico, everywhere. Competition nights attract the fastest feet in town; also the fastest drinkers.... *Tel 0171/379–3277. 96 Charing Cross Rd. WC2, Leicester Square tube stop. Open till 2am. Closed Sun. Cover charge.*

Shepherds Bush Empire. A medium-to-big—no, make that a big—venue for bands you've heard of even if you're over forty. Though it's not unhip. Book ahead, usually.... *Tel 0181/740–7474. Shepherds Bush Green W10, Shepherds Bush tube stop. Cover charge.*

606. A great jazz boîte with round tables and a stage, real food, and a reliably wholehearted atmosphere, thanks to the fine acts it books. It's more of a supper club than a nightclub or a straight-up music venue. A bit hidden away in the Fulham backwaters.... *Tel 0171/352–5953. 90 Lots Rd. SW10, Fulham Broadway tube stop. Open till 2am. Closed some days (call). Cover charge.*

Soho House. Another members-only Soho haunt of media types. Groucho's much-newer rival, appealing more to the advertising/PR/video producing type.... *Tel 0171/734–5188. 40 Greek St. W1, Leicester Square tube stop. Members and guests only.*

Station Tavern. This is a pub, from its whirly pattern, smoke-marinated carpet to its old geezers sipping a pint in the corner. There's an R&B band every night, and what they lack in slickness, they make up for in enthusiasm. A good time was had by all, especially the urban anthropologists.... *Tel 0171/727–4053. 41 Bramley Rd. W10, Latimer Road tube stop. Open pub hours.*

Subterania. A groovy duplex dive beneath the Westway in Notting Hill hosts happening bands—very often not homegrown ones—and does weekend clubbing for seriously cool and beautiful twenties.... *Tel 0181/960–4590. 12 Acklam Rd., Ladbroke Grove tube stop. Open till 3:30am. Cover charge.*

Triñanes. Where everyone goes when turfed out of the Forum across the street. The tapas—let alone the Spanish entrées—are not why, but the flamenco performers downstairs are a weekend plus.... *Tel 0171/482–3616. 298 Kentish Town Rd. NW5, Kentish Town tube stop. Open till 2am. Closed Sun.*

Twelve Bar Club. As you'd expect, this is a blues-centric place, and one with a consistently wonderful atmosphere and simpatico management, too.... *Tel 0171/916–6989. Denmark Place, Denmark St. WC2, Tottenham Court Road tube stop. Cover charge.*

United Kingdom. Granted permission to expand at press time, this was already one of the more capacious clubs in London. Club UK hit the headlines in 1995 for a fatal "E" mishap, and is the nearest thing to one of those legendary illegal warehouse raves you read about in the late eighties.... *Tel 0181/877–0110. Buckhold Rd. SW18, Wandsworth Town tube stop. Open till 6am. Closed some days (call). Cover charge.*

The Vine. Very near the big and popular Forum, this is a contrasting thing—a pub that has various folkie styles of musicians performing, emphasis on the Gaelic.... *Tel 0171/ 209–0038. 86 Highgate Rd. NW5, Kentish Town tube stop. Open pub hours. Cover charge most nights.*

Vortex. Serious jazz buffs should make the trek out to Stokey— a residential neighborhood, with Asian vegetarian restaurants and some good pubs—for the cutting edge of the London scene.... *Tel 0171/254–6516. Stoke Newington Church St., Stoke Newington BR.*

The Wag. A very long-running Soho club indeed, the three-floor Wag has notably variable vibes, and is perhaps more prone to have an off-night than a newer venue—though it also manages to hit the jackpot over and over again. Check the listings; ask around.... *Tel 0171/437–5534. 35–37 Wardour St. W1, Piccadilly Circus tube stop. Open till 6am. Closed some days (call). Cover charge.*

Waxy O'Connor's. Big enough to contain part of a Dublin street, a bit of cathedral, and a fully grown tree, this bar's as Irish as Demis Roussos, but it's fun.... *Tel 0171/287–0255. Rupert St. W1, Piccadilly Circus tube stop. Open pub hours.*

Weavers. Past the Garage in the far north, this is the folkie pub par excellence, worth the trek for country-billies, steel guitarists, Cajuns, and seekers after the English sound.... *Tel 0171/226–6911. 98 Newington Green Rd. N1, Highbury and Islington tube stop. Open till midnight some nights. Cover charge.*

Wembley Arena. A big, big venue for big, big bands, way the hell out.... *Tel 0181/900–1234. Empire Way, Wembley, Middlesex, Wembley Park tube stop. Admission charge.*

Wembley Stadium. An even bigger venue for even bigger bands.... *Tel 0181/900–1234. Empire Way, Wembley, Middlesex. Wembley Park tube stop. Admission charge.*

Whirl-Y-Gig. A total anomaly when it started, this New Age, non-ageist party has become hip despite itself, with a slew of similar floaty-hippie-shamanic-rave-ups following in its footsteps. Music is ambient-to-house, with live bands also, and props include oil-wheel lights, balloons, and a giant parachute dropped over the dance floor.... *Tel 0181/864–6760. Shoreditch Town Hall N1, Old Street tube stop. Open till midnight. Up to two nights a week only (call). Cover charge.*

WKD Music Café. A glass shopfront next to Sainsbury's supermarket in Camden, with big letters fashioned from wrought iron, is the uninviting frontage, but once inside this bar/café, the feel is warm and the music sometimes red-hot—especially in the popular jam sessions.... *Tel 0171/267–1869. 18 Kentish Town Rd. NW1, Camden Town tube stop. Open till 2am. Cover charge most nights.*

Central London Clubs

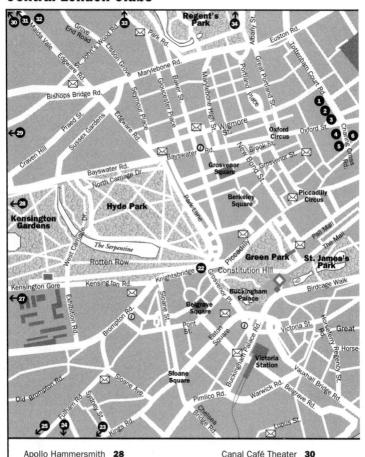

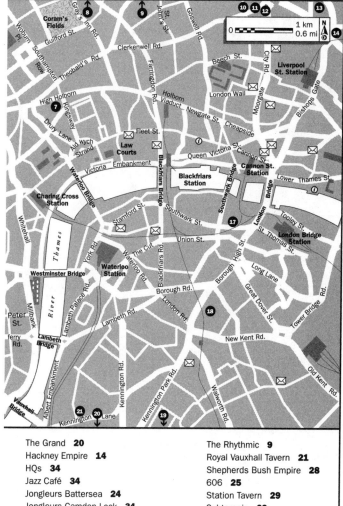

The Grand **20**
Hackney Empire **14**
HQs **34**
Jazz Café **34**
Jongleurs Battersea **24**
Jongleurs Camden Lock **34**
King's Head **9**
Loughborough Hotel **19**
Mars **5**
Mean Fiddler **33**
Ministry of Sound **18**
The National **32**
The Office **2**
Pizza on the Park **22**

The Rhythmic **9**
Royal Vauxhall Tavern **21**
Shepherds Bush Empire **28**
606 **25**
Station Tavern **29**
Subterania **29**
Twelve Bar Club **6**
United Kingdom **24**
The Vine **34**
Vortex **9**
Weavers **9**
Wembley Arena/Stadium **31**
Whirl-Y-Gig **13**
WKD Music Café **34**

Mayfair, St. James's & Piccadilly Clubs

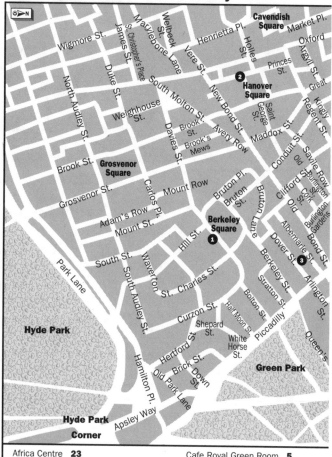

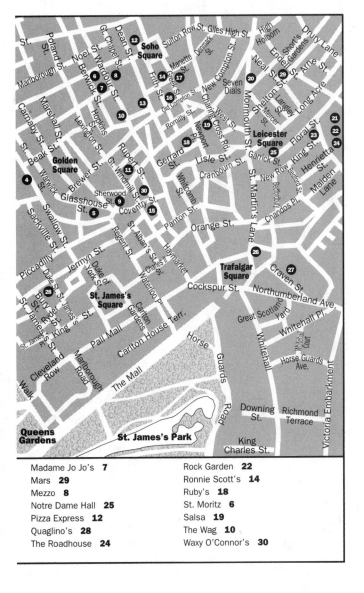

Madame Jo Jo's **7**	Rock Garden **22**
Mars **29**	Ronnie Scott's **14**
Mezzo **8**	Ruby's **18**
Notre Dame Hall **25**	St. Moritz **6**
Pizza Express **12**	Salsa **19**
Quaglino's **28**	The Wag **10**
The Roadhouse **24**	Waxy O'Connor's **30**

the bar

scene 2

Alcohol is not the only
fuel for a good time, of
course, but Londoners—
well, the British in
general—prefer a wet bar
to a juice bar. The great
British pub, or public

house, ideally offers exactly what its title implies—a warm environment where many people feel at home. However, great changes have occurred in the traditional hostelry during the past decade. Pubs used to have sawdust or faded linoleum, a dart board, an indoor fog of smoke, and no women. Now half of them are bars with cappuccino machines and sofas, and the other half are quasi-restaurants. This, of course, has led to nostalgia for the grotty old dives we shunned, and some of London's grooviest watering holes are unreconstructed old geezers' pubs that have been seized upon in fits of reverse snobbery.

Any discussion of London drinking venues must begin with an explanation of the arcane alcohol-licensing laws. If you're British, 11pm becomes ingrained in the body as the time the average evening out winds down, because that's when the bar shuts. The "last orders" bell, rung in pubs at 10:50, and the "time" bell have created many an alcoholic, trained to chugalug several pints before curfew. The law came in as a measure to increase wartime production. That's the first World War. Yes, the ridiculous drinking hours were set in 1915, and, despite near-universal unpopularity, persist today. The law bends more these days, though, and late licenses are becoming more common, with more places enabled to let you drink till midnight, or even later on weekends. Separate laws always did apply to private clubs, restaurants, and places with a cover charge. Most restaurants serve alcohol to diners until midnight or 1am; there's another kind of restuarant where you can arrive after midnight and drink as long as you eat as well. Most choices in Late Night Dining fall into one of these two categories.

The Beaten Path

Soho is the place to bar-crawl in central London, with all variety of drinking den back-to-back within a few blocks, and plenty of late-night places, albeit ones that charge cover. Other neighborhoods for concentrated bar-hopping are Camden and Notting Hill, with Chelsea/Fulham providing a more spread-out bar buffet. Camden goes in and out of favor as top trendy place, while Notting Hill has been pretty persistently hip since the sixties. Chelsea is now and always has been for the trust-fund set.

What To Order

British beer is world-famous, and bitter is the indigenous brew. Despite the best efforts of the 25-year-old Campaign for Real Ale (CAMRA), many British prefer highly carbonated bastard drinks—European bottled lagers, big brewery beers, extra-strong hard cider ("cider" here always means hard—the other stuff is apple juice), alcoholic lemonades. Traditionally brewed real bitter is top-fermented ale that's been fermented a second time in a wooden barrel—hence the term "cask ale." It tastes of hops and barley, is practically fizz-free, and is served warm or at cellar temperature, pulled from the tap in pints. Purists often ask for their "pint of best" in a "straight glass" instead of the default glass—a heavy tankard with a handle.

The big breweries own most of the small beer names, much like giant publishing companies own the smaller imprints, meaning that many of the taps you see in the pub draw mere simulacrums of British bitter. An exception is the Allied Lyons–owned Firkin chain, started by beer visionary David Bruce, and still brewing Dogbolter, Rail Ale, and sundry site-specific specials in the cellars of the roughly 25 London Firkins. Elsewhere, order ales by Young's or Fuller's—the two major independent breweries left in the capital. Young's has its ordinary and its special, the latter being deeper, darker, maltier, and stronger, at 4.6% alcohol. Fuller's brews are Chiswick ("ordinary"), London Pride ("best"), and ESB ("extra special bitter"), with a hefty 5.5% alcohol. Otherwise, go to the brewpub **The Orange Brewery** in Pimlico, or somewhere that specializes in real ales, like **The Sun** in Bloomsbury, with 16 taps. If pennies are scant, seek out a J. D. Wetherspoon, identifiable by lack of music, smoke-free zones, and cheap (£1-ish) pints of Younger's.

As for other beers, the Irish Guinness is everywhere, but the even thicker and blacker stout, Murphy's, is gaining ground, and there are a million lagers, from Sweden, Prague, Mexico, Transylvania—you name it—on tap, bottled, lite, extra-strong, etc., plus Trappist beers and Weissbier and wheat beer—and so on. Beer cocktails are a sure route to hangover city: A Snakebite is half-beer, half-cider (hard); a Black Velvet is Guinness and champagne; a Black and Tan is half stout, half bitter; and a Depth Charge is a pint of bitter with a shot glass of crème de menthe dropped in it, glass and all (honestly). The British do like beer.

Wine is also liked, though it's not usually worth ordering in a pub. Enologists should stick to the few wine bars that remain from the 1960s and 1970s. New ones are rare. As for hard liquor, you'll be shocked at the tiny puddle that is one

LONDON ⌒ THE BAR SCENE

measure of spirits, dispensed from the "optic" attached to an upside-down bottle. Apart from a spirit with a mixer—gin and tonic, for instance—pubs don't tend to offer cocktails. For those, you'll need a bar. Maybe the vogue for melting things in vodka will be over by now, but if not, order a shot of Mars Bar, white Toblerone, wine gum, banana, or toffee vodka, and good luck to you.

Etiquette

In pubs, don't tip the bartender, and don't sit at the bar with your cash in a pile and expect him to peel off the right amount. The barkeep isn't going to buy you a drink either, although you might offer him one ("and have one for yourself," you might say). When drinking in a group of two to six or so, it's customary for one person to stand a round for everyone—a favor reciprocated by each person in turn, except for the cheapskate who disappears to the bathroom whenever glasses empty. The bathroom is "the loo," "the ladies," or "the gents."

As you already know, drink-up, get-out time anywhere without a special license is 11pm, or 10:30 on Sundays, and wherever The Index states "pub hours" this is what to expect. You may stumble on a "lock-in," if you're drinking with a regular outside central London. This is the illegal practice whereby the pub landlord literally locks the door on the remaining customers, and continues serving alcohol. Often, pubs that do "afters" have a policeman regular providing unofficial insurance. Carding is virtually unknown in London, even though a place can be shut down for allowing under-18s to drink alcohol. Still, if you look young, do carry ID. Carry a gas mask also, if you're smoke-sensitive. Although not quite as bad as Paris or Rome, London isn't called "the Old Smoke" for nothing.

The Lowdown

Personality pubs... In the eighties, the big breweries (landlords of most pubs) converted nearly every dear old down-home barroom into small Edwardian theme parks, with antiquarian books by the mile, fake log fires, brass rails, and stuffed owls. The nineties ethos replaced Ye Olde Curiosity Pub with bare floorboards, sofas, coffee, vodka shots, and bruschetta. But what do you do when you want the hokey old traditional pub experience—and what visitor wouldn't, at least once? Best not start at **Ye Olde Cheshire Cheese** on Fleet Street, which, though it is a genuine 330 years olde, is terribly touristy. On the other hand, its sawdust floors, low, wood-beamed ceilings, and 14th-century crypt are just the same as when Dickens drank there. Don't get too excited by that last part. Either Dickens drank nearly everywhere in London or publicans are congenital liars. Among those claiming the serial novelist are **The George Inn**, south of the Thames, which he featured in *Little Dorritt*, and which is worth patronizing for its gallery and courtyard; **Jack Straw's Castle**, out Hampstead way, where he'd stay the night but you can just enjoy the garden (the reconstructed pub itself isn't much); the neighboring **The Spaniards Inn**, with another garden; and **The Lamb**, which was actually his local when he lived at what's now his museum. He didn't go to **The French House**, where the Resistance convened during WWII, and where they still don't serve English pints. It's been a Soho institution for years, as has **The Coach and Horses**, which had a long-running play about one regular—soused *Spectator* magazine columnist Jeffrey Bernard—set there. It's a belly-up-to-the-bar dive, unlike the following. Back up north, Islington's **The Albion** has a cute garden, blackened beams, and nooks whose coziness is surpassed only by the Hampstead **Holly Bush**, practically unchanged since the 17th century, and its contemporary, the Highgate **Flask**, which is like a country pub on the village green.

Historic pubs... Most of the above qualify on this count too, especially the first two and the last two. But history groupies might trek to the 17th-century riverside **Mayflower**, named after *that* Mayflower, and marking the virtual spot from which the pilgrim fathers set sail. **The Cittie of Yorke** looks like history itself, with its soaring heraldic Gothic hall, hundred-mile bar, and big butts—vast, iron-hooped wooden wine vats—lined up on the gallery. At the other end of High Holborn is another gorgeous article, **The Princess Louise**, which has the only gent's bathroom we know to be graced by a preservation order. It is high Victorian, as is the pub, with ceramic tiles and marble pillars, polished brass, etched glass, and mahogany paneling. The oldest riverside inn is not the George or the Mayflower, but **The Prospect of Whitby**, founded in 1520 way out in Wapping. It's worth visiting for its terrace, its flagstone bar, and its neighborhood of narrow winding alleys between (mostly) restored Victorian warehouses, off the tourist trail.

Grunge pubs... The **Warwick Castle** smells like teen bedrooms, and would be the ideal pit if it weren't for the quantity of white guys with dreadlocks. The Camden Town **Devonshire Arms** ("Dev") and the former old soaks' haven, **The Good Mixer**, are also pleasantly lowlife, but too full of people who know each other. Camden's shabbiest, finest pub was the permanently half-empty Mother Red Cap, a cavern of an Irish tavern that's been transmogrified into the **World's End**, into which under-20s now stack themselves in layers. Nearby, **The Black Cap**, prime drag cabaret stage, has always been nice and sleazy, as has **The French House**, lined with boxing photos, serving no pints, flying the "tricolor" over Dean Street, as always, though it's too well-known to be any kind of find; ditto **The Coach and Horses**, which has made a little industry out of its grungehood. The best grunge pub is the one you stumble into steps away from where you're staying, but for grunge lite, try **The Cow** (see Late Night Dining), which is styled precisely like an ancient inn on the Liffey but has surreptitious designer detailing, or the nearby **Ground Floor**, which attempts the post-apocalyptic look.

Real ale... Some ales are realer than others, and none is real-er than Pimlico Porter from the Victorian-style **Orange Brewery**. Take a £3 tour of the basement brewery, and sup a free half-pint as you check out exactly how real it is. Also try the SW1 and SW2 brews. Ask nicely, and you may get invited to tour the cellars of **The Sun**, though this one has only other people's ales, albeit many of them—Ruddles, Tanglefoot, Adnams, Wadsworth—have names to glad-den the hearts of country folk. At any of the pubs with "Firkin" in its name, you can have a pint of Rail Ale, Dogbolter, or the appropriately named "house brew." The newish theaterland **Flyman and Firkin**, for instance, has a Critics Ale and a Flyman (that's the guy who flies the scenery out) Bitter, while **The Ferret and Firkin** has Ferret Ale. Firkins tend to attract a frat-type crowd, as does any beer-centric place, and this is especially true at the biggest, **The Pharaoh and Firkin**. For the good Irish stout, **Minogues** is more salubrious than the *echt* Irish pubs along the Kilburn High Road, pours Murphy's, and usually has live music, but **O'Hanlons** is the real thing. John O'Hanlon imports his Guinness from Dublin, and brews his own O'Hanlons. Irish Ale, too, which you can sup out back in the covered yard. **Waxy O'Connor's**, the Irish theme bar, with confession box and pulpit, growing tree, and Dublin street inside, does surprisingly well on the beer; it has Murphy's, Guinness, and Beamish on tap (see Late Night Dining).

Martinis... The **American Bar** at the Savoy (jacket and tie required) claims to have introduced this ultimate cocktail to London at least, and maybe to the world, so it ought to be good—and it is. Best mixed nuts in town, too. The other classic, uptown place to imbibe is the newly trendy **Café Royal**; the lesser-known place with one of the best bar staff in town is **The Gore Bar**, next door to Bistrot 190, which is actually an after-work club for chefs and restaurateurs, and is good and dark, with sofas and booths and a long line of bar stools for perching. Drop into **Quaglino's** (see Late Night Dining) for a "Vodkatini" en route to eating or dancing somewhere else, and you'll get the best of the glamorous space and the view over the din-ers in captivity. You have to be a captive diner yourself to do the **Atlantic** thing on a weekend, but don't bother, because the only safe area in there for a correct martini is the intimate Dick's Bar, named for Dick Bradsell, who left to open **Flamingo**—also a martini/Manhattan/mimosa sort of place.

Rum, cognac, single malts... Do not, repeat not, slump on one of the Lanesborough's plush leather chesterfields at **The Library** and ask Salvatore Calabrese for a brandy alexander. It's his life's passion to collect historic cognac, bottled during years when something big happened—liquid history, going for up to £500 a shot. There are more sofas in the cute, petite **Whisky Bar** at the Atheneum hotel in Piccadilly, which you'll need if you take up their Passport invitation—a special deal on every one of their 70 single malts, Irish whiskeys, bourbons, and whatnot. You get a free bottle if you're still alive at the end. The many tropical liquids at **Cottons Rhum Shop** are available undiluted by fruit pulp. Best order some "Long Mouth Doris" (a dish of garlic shrimp and mussels) with that, so you get a more comfy table in the dark interior, though the reggae bass boom is fierce. For a similar effect, faster **Waxy O'Connor's** serves a version of the illegal (when home-brewed) Irish potato liquor, poteen, but the drink endemic to this city is flavored vodka. Get your marshmallow, chili or vanilla, licorice or cantaloupe shots at: **Ground Floor**, **Mars** (see The Club Scene), **Riki-Tik**, **babushka**, **The Edge**, or **Freedom**, to name a few.

Long sloe comfortable screws... Places to drink this, and frozen margaritas, and sickly things with cream and kahlua, are few, and, as you'd expect, they tend to have a singles bent. **Le Shaker at Nam Long** has a sign that claims: "Golden, Classic and Exotic Cocktails at its best in Chelsea." **Beach Blanket Babylon** and its young sibling, fetchingly titled **Mwah Mwah** (as in kiss kiss), both mix a mean Long Island iced tea, and can whip up a frenzied pink lady. **Trader Vic's**—yes, there is one in London—does what it does with "Tiki Puka Pukas," while the **Flamingo** does the posh version, mixed by Dick Bradsell and crew in Hawaiian shirts, and coming out better than they do at Dick's last place, **The Atlantic** (even counting his eponymous bar). Proving that funny cocktails aren't beneath you, **Riki-Tik** does a whole gamut, starring disgusting ones made with flavored vodkas, and—proving that they are—**Break for the Border** dispenses pomegranate or almond margaritas, slammers, and those "Long Sloe Comfortable Screws" (Long Island iced tea with sloe gin and Southern Comfort). The best island-style cocktails are at **Cottons Rhum Shop**, where you can have "Sex in the Bush" in a tropical shanty interior.

OJ and cappuccino... You can get nonalcoholic beverages anyplace, but there tends to be a distinct line drawn between a dry place and a wet bar in London, a historic circumstance that grew from those licensing laws. These places blur the line. It's lovely to spend time in the **Living Room**, reading the stacks of newsprint, eavesdropping on the well-to-do arty people, loafing. Close by is buzzy **Bar Italia** (see Late Night Dining) for a stand-up espresso on the way home or out. Get a table at **The Elbow Room**— a pool table—or at **Café Bohème** for coffee and tart and you won't need a drink, nor will you at the **Angel Café Bar**, a gay hangout where the "Angel Smoothie" is the thing to order. **The Edge** has both coffee and flavored vodkas, and a very mixed crowd that gets more testosterone-oriented the nearer the weekend and the later it is. **Cyberia Cyber Café** has Web browsers where other bars have beers.

Cruising, schmoozing, meeting (straight)... A designated singles scene really doesn't exist in London, because the unwritten rules of dating are not the same here. Exactly how, we couldn't say (these are *unwritten* rules), but see if you notice a difference at **Beach Blanket Babylon**, where the decor is suitably Gothic for the throbbing mass of young people convening on weekend nights, especially in summer. **Mwah Mwah** is doing similar trade in Chelsea, where teens have more money but less style, and are the most apt to go out cruising. Chelsea specializes in annoying names, if that and **Po-Na-Na** constitute a trend. This steamy basement souk bar is a posey, slightly model-y pickup scene, while nearby **Kartouche**'s basement bar is a posey, model-y, Eurotrashy pickup scene. Get the difference? If not, go to **Come the Revolution**, which *was* the Chelsea posey, model-y, Eurotrashy pickup scene, but is now just a pickup scene. So is the bizarre **Le Shaker at Nam Long**, with its live fish trapped in glass pillars downstairs. Now head north to left-wing, arty, rather serious Islington, where older guys hang at **The**

Island Queen (next to the house where playwright Joe Orton lived with, and was murdered by, Ken Halliwell), where pool table, jukebox, and clientele all smoke. Young Islingtonians, who are nearly all actors, are too laid-back to cruise at the funky **Medicine Bar**. The classic neighborhood hangout, go-home-together pubs are the incredibly seedy **Warwick Castle** on Portobello Road, and the mystifyingly ordinary **Devonshire Arms** and hideous **Good Mixer** in Camden. If you can get into the **Groucho**, you'll certainly see chatting-up in progress, though, despite being named after the man who didn't want a club that would take him, the most famous media-movie-journo hangout is liable to ignore you unless it knows you. All you need to get attention at the younger membership-only place around the corner, **Soho House**, however, is a short skirt and a seat at the circular bar on a weekend. For a taste of the old frat house, go **Break for the Border** and slam tequila.

Cruising, schmoozing, meeting (gay)... The earth revolves around "the Compton"—Soho's always-lively Old Compton Street, which underwent metamorphosis sometime this decade and is now almost New York-y in its hours and its up-frontness. As we've said, places mostly welcome a mix (permutations of gay/straight/men/women), but men are the target customers of **Freedom Café Bar** and **The Village**. Biggest and busiest is probably that and **The Yard**, followed by much smaller **The Edge**, which gets packed out on weekend nights, while little **First Out** peacefully purveys caffeine. The dyke scene doesn't really center on Soho, nor on any one place, though you can count on any and every women-only event attracting mostly gay women. The West End arts center, the **Drill Hall**, runs loads of these, plus it has a popular girls' bar night Mondays. **The Box** has its Girl Bar Sundays (see The Club Scene), while the **Angel Café Bar** has girls every night, although it's officially a gay bar for both genders. **The Royal Vauxhall Tavern**, where London's first amateur drag cabaret is still going, is more for men, but there is a women's night, too, and there are usually some straight people muscling in on the scene. That's also true of Camden's **Black Cap**, which has the best drag queen lip-synching cabaret of all and stays open late.

Late, later... In Soho, **Bar Sol Ona** (Barcelona, ha ha), and its neighbor, **Café Bohème**, both let you drink till midnight, though neither has much else to recommend it beyond that. **The Edge** is gay-oriented and open nearly all night, but stops with the alcohol around 1am, as does nearby **Riki-Tik**. Careful there though—one of the owners confided that Riki-Tik is so damn hip even *she* sometimes feels out of place. **Mars** gives us only one extra hour in its three cozy floors of mosaic tiles and plaster stalactites, but it's a rare hour for Covent Garden (see The Club Scene). Going west, Chelsea is well set up for drinkers, with most of the places on the pickup circuit staying open at least an extra hour—**Po-Na-Na**, **Kartouche**, and **Le Shaker** among them. A candidate for most sordid late-night dive in town is the compulsory stop-in-after-the-Forum **Triñanes** (see The Club Scene), a Spanish restaurant (don't eat here) catercorner from that Kentish Town hall of rock. Still north, in Islington, the **Medicine Bar** is licensed till midnight, and is full of old couches for lounging.

Latest... The **Atlantic** transformed central London's nights with its revolutionary 3am closing time. Unfortunately, at press time it still lacks a whole lot of competition. The latest late place should have opened by now, though, and is promising. Ed Baines, ex-chef at Daphne's (see Late Night Dining) is among those behind this "classical" (his word) salon for dressing up, eating and drinking in a former porn cinema opposite Madame Jo Jo's. Round here is also **Mezzo** (see Late Night Dining), the biggest restaurant in Europe, whose two bars are open till 3am weekends, but where you can't just drink, and the **Groucho**, where you can't even do that unless you're with a member. Even with a member, Groucho closes at a paltry 1am, whereupon everyone decamps to the **Soho House** until 3—if they know a member. In Soho without members, you'll have to pay cover to patronize **Little Italy's** overlit restaurant-bar until 3am, sibling of next-door **Bar Italia** (see Late Night Dining for both establishments), where you can drink all night—as long as it's espresso and San Pelligrino. Elsewhere in the West End, the rowdiest late-night drinking den—and that's no compliment—is **Break for the Border**; the coolest is **Flamingo**, an Atlantic off-shoot and cocktail bar of the moment circa 1996, with lounge music that gets too loud for talking later on. **Rocky's** is open till 3am, and that's the best feature of this rather odd, sport-themed chrome-and-neon bar. The longest hours of all are at the bright and reasonably priced **Vingt-Quatre**—24 hours, as the name suggests (see Late Night Dining). Also at **The Columbia**, if you're friends with whatever band is staying in the hotel upstairs.

Dives... A dive must have made no attempt to decorate and must deliver nil attitude while making you feel pleasantly sleazy. Try **Bradley's** when up west. It's a cramped Spanish bar, unchanged since Franco, with booths beneath the arches in the basement, castanets and bullfight posters, and student architects from the Architectural Association down the block. **Triñanes**, of course, is the leading skeevy Spanish bar (see The Club Scene), though **Bar Sol Ona** is trying for the crown. None of the newer bars is a dive, except maybe **Mars** (see The Club Scene), which isn't too posey, and also **The Living Room**, despite being handsome, with its floorboards and sofas, and despite having no alcohol license. In Islington, **Minogues** has aged its way into this category, although it'll never be as Irish as **O'Hanlons**. Near there, in the King's Cross wasteland beside the Grand Union Canal, is **The Waterside**, which is perfectly salubrious, with its lovely terrace on the Battlebridge Basin, but still manages to suggest white-trash values. The louchest bar is the one at **The Columbia**, on a good night; off-peak, it's merely drab. **The Ring**'s swirly carpets, formica, vinyl, fakewood veneer, fight posters, photos of boxers, and no trendies whatsoever add up to grunge perfection.

For good sports... Places to play pool are at a premium on weekend nights, and you should set out early, get your money down, and be a good player (the winner stays on and plays the next game). **Ye Olde Swiss Cottage** was beautifully vile and style-free until they dressed it up in faux Victoriana, but the six-table pool club in back is still fine. **The Raj** in Holland Park is also worth patronizing, but only for the tables (it has five)—luckily, both of these are steps from the tube. **The Elbow Room** is the first non-pub, non-club pool haunt, with eight tables dressed in dove gray. Sports bars are not a London phenomenon, but there are a couple of U.S.-style newcomers. Cricketer

Victor Ubogu opened swanky **Shoeless Joe's** with Christopher Gilmour of Christopher's (see Late Night Dining) in 1995. Upstairs in the restaurant, the TVs don't speak, but there's a wall-size screen in the basement bar. Shoeless Joe's is to **The Sports Café** as baseball is to hockey, and this 120-screen, three-bar megapub is appropriately bankrolled by Labatt's. **Rocky's** is a useful late-late alternative—the place to catch the 2am main event from Vegas, but fight fans should enter **The Ring** for the true flavor of British boxing. It took up the slack from the old Thomas à Becket, the pugilists' pub for decades, currently closed. There's a gym upstairs, where publican Neville Axford trains his fighters.

For balmy evenings... Some of the best pub gardens are found up north. **The Freemason's Arms**, **The Spaniards Inn**, and **Jack Straw's Castle** are Hampstead's finest, all steps away from the Heath. Over in Islington, **The Albion**'s beer garden has trailing plants on trellises and a crowd, while Highgate has the front yard of **The Flask**, which is about the only London garden with space heaters. Notting Hill environs boast **The Windsor Castle**, which has one of the cutest walled gardens in town, but good luck squeezing in, and **The Cow**, which, with its across-the-street rival, **The Westbourne** (see Late Night Dining for both), appropriates the extended sidewalk for outside drinking all summer long. Further west, **Come the Revolution** has a pretty patio ringed with frescoes, and there are plenty of sidewalk tables around—like at the friendly pub that was hip in the 1960s and 1970s, **The Chelsea Potter**. Sidewalk tables are ubiquitous in town, too, but Lamb's Conduit Street outside **The Lamb** is always thronged by a post-work crowd just standing around. **The Yard** has a courtyard in Soho. For waterside drinking, by all means try **The Prospect of Whitby**'s or **The Mayflower**'s terraces, but don't make them your sole reason for the endless trek. **The Waterside** has a good lesser-known terrace on an obscure basin for barges and houseboats that's a short walk from King's Cross.

The Index

The Albion. The epitome of the cute neighborhood pub—we wish. Garden in back, tables out front, open fires, nooks, beams, and weekend crowds.... *Tel 0171/607-7450. 10 Thornhill Rd. N1, Angel tube stop. Open pub hours.*

The American Bar. Did they invent the martini here, or do they just act that way? Don't forget the tie, guys.... *Tel 0171/ 836-4343. Savoy Hotel, Strand WC2, Aldwych tube stop. Open pub hours.*

Angel Café Bar. Laid-back and continental by day, cruisier by night, this gay place is more dykey than queeny.... *Tel 0171/608-2656. 65 Graham St. N1, Angel tube stop. Open Mon–Sat noon–midnight, pub hours Sun.*

The Atlantic. Boasting the first central late-late alcohol without cover, this subterranean ocean liner is more the restaurant now, with velvet rope for plebes without dinner reservations or a close relationship to the owners... *Tel 0171/734-4888. 20 Glasshouse St. W1, Piccadilly Square tube stop. Open Mon–Sat 12pm–3am, Sun 6–10:30pm.*

babushka. En route to the Ministry of Sound or the South Bank, stop for a licorice vodka amid acres of floorboard and mural; food, too.... *Tel 0171/928-3693; 173 Blackfriars Rd. SE1, Waterloo tube stop. Open Thu, Fri 12pm–12am; Sat 7pm–midnight; pub hours Mon–Wed.*

Bar Sol Ona. A touristy Spanish-style bar with tapas, useful for being Soho-central and staying open late.... *Tel 0171/287-9432. 13 Old Compton St. W1, Leicester Square tube stop. Open 7pm–midnight.*

Beach Blanket Babylon. As a place to cruise fellow 20s and 30s, this touristique Portobello joint rocks on weekends. Looks like Gaudí collaborated with Dali.... *Tel 0171/229–2907. 45 Ledbury Rd. W11, Notting Hill Gate tube stop. Open pub hours.*

The Black Cap. Along with the Royal Vauxhall Tavern, this is the homespun bedrock of drag cabaret, home of the lip synch, steamy purveyor of glam.... *Tel 0171/485–1742. 171 Camden High St. NW1, Camden Town tube stop. Open Mon–Thur 1pm–2am; Fri, Sat till 3am; till midnight Sun.*

Bradley's. An old Spanish bar with a Moorish dungeon of a basement, beloved of local architectural students.... *Tel 0171/636–0359. 42–44 Hanway St. W1, Tottenham Court Rd. tube stop. Open pub hours.*

Break for the Border. Frat-boy types slam tequilas to loud live generic rock and soul.... *Tel 0171/437–8595. 5 Goslett Yard WC2, Tottenham Court Road tube stop. Open Mon–Wed 5:30pm–1am, Thu–Sat till 3am, Sun till 11pm.*

Café Bohème. This well-bred, Parisian-style corner brasserie mutates into a standing-room-only free-for-all when the pubs decant into it at 11pm, at which point cover is charged.... *Tel 0171/734–0623. 13 Old Compton St. W1, Leicester Square tube stop. Open Mon–Sat 8am–3am, Sun 10am–10:30pm.*

Café Royal. The dress-up, martini-with-an-olive, table-service bar, with cabaret next door in the Green Room.... *Tel 0171/437–9090. 68 Regent St. W1, Piccadilly Circus tube stop. Open pub hours Mon–Sat, Sun noon–3pm.*

The Chelsea Potter. A neighborhood fave since at least the 1950s—for antique traders, teddy boys, punks, and all. Summer sidewalk tables are prime.... *Tel 0171/352–9479. 119 King's Rd. SW3, Sloane Sq. tube stop. Open pub hours.*

The Cittie of Yorke. Gorgeous are the neo-Gothic acres of this Sam Smith (who makes good brews) pub—one of London's finest.... *Tel 0171/242-7670. 22 High Holborn WC1, Holborn tube stop. Open pub hours Mon–Sat.*

The Coach and Horses. A tiny, smoky, ugly dive of a Soho pub is famous for being Jeffrey Barnard's local—the place that made him too "unwell" to pen his *Spectator* column. All pubs used to look like this.... *Tel 0171/437–5920. 29 Greek St. W1, Leicester Square tube stop. Open pub hours.*

The Columbia. Beautifully style-free hotel bar replete with rock 'n' roll raunch and seediness.... *Tel 0171/402–0021. 95-99 Lancaster Gate W2, Lancaster Gate tube stop. Open pub hours for nonguests.*

Come the Revolution. At the difficult end of the King's Road, this had Eurotrash, which passed on, leaving the dungeon decor and nice garden for us.... *Tel 0171/384–3061. 541 King's Rd. SW6, Fulham Broadway tube stop. Open pub hours.*

Cottons Rhum Shop. Camden's Caribbean island. Has the best rum drinks and hottest jerked chicken.... *Tel 0171/482–1096. 55 Chalk Farm Rd. NW1, Chalk Farm tube stop. Open till midnight.*

Cyberia Cyber Café. Log on, tune out, drop off.... *Tel 0171/209–0982. E-mail: cyberia@easynet.co.uk. 39 Whitfield St. W1, Goodge Street tube stop. Open Mon–Fri 11am–10pm; Sat, Sun 10am–9pm.*

The Devonshire Arms. Camden's original cliquey, ugly pub, whose appeal may escape you.... *Tel 0171/485–2079. 33 Kentish Town Rd. NW1, Camden Town tube stop. Open pub hours.*

Drill Hall. In deep West End, this woman-centric arts center runs many a girlish event, and does a women-only bar Mondays.... *Tel 0171/631–1353. 16 Chenies St. W1, Goodge Street tube stop. Cover charge most nights.*

The Edge. On the edge of Soho, this gay bar is often jumping through the night, though the most flavored vodkas in the world go off-line at 1am.... *Tel 0171/439–1313. 11 Soho Sq. W1, Tottenham Court Road tube stop. Open Mon–Sat noon–1am, Sun noon–10:30pm.*

The Elbow Room. For shooting pool (see Sports)....*Tel 0171/221–5211. 103 Westbourne Grove W2, Bayswater tube stop. Open noon–11:30pm.*

The Ferret and Firkin. You'll see Firkin pubs everywhere, all of them with wooden church pews on bare floorboards, serving Firkin puns, Dogbolter ale brewed on-site, and live music. This one's by the river in Chelsea, and is lousy with locals.... *Tel 0171/352–6645. 114 Lots Rd. SW10, Fulham Broadway tube stop. Open pub hours.*

First Out. The name is exact—if you're walking into Soho from the direction of Oxford Street, and are gay, the relaxed and friendly cafe is the first landmark.... *Tel 0171/240–8042. 52 St. Giles High St. W1, Tottenham Court Road tube stop.*

Flamingo. Dick Bradsell—of Dick's Bar at the Atlantic, and before that, Fred's (which predates Groucho as the trendy-club)—is king of the cocktail cult, and the beautiful young love his place.... *Tel 0171/493–0689. 9 Hanover St. W1, Oxford Circus tube stop. Open Mon–Fri 5.30pm–3am, Sat 8pm–3am.*

The Flask. An exact simulacrum of the village pub, with beams, fireplaces, and a big yard in front.... *Tel 0181/340–7260. 77 Highgate West Hill N6, Highgate tube stop. Open pub hours.*

The Flyman and Firkin. One of the newer Firkins, though you'd never know, looking at its aged wood and brick. It's theater-land, so order Critics Ale.... *Tel 0171/240–7109. 166–170 Shaftsbury Ave. WC2, Leicester Sq. tube stop. Open pub hours Mon–Sat.*

Freedom Café Bar. The most posey and, latterly, cruisey of Soho's new bar breed.... *Tel 0171/734–0071. 60-66 Wardour St. W1, Leicester Sq. tube stop. Open 9am–3am (cover after 11pm).*

The Freemason's Arms. On the edge of the Heath, this has one of the biggest pub gardens in town, which is overrun with the local, wealthy brand of teenager on summer week-ends.... *Tel 0171/435–4498. 32 Downshire Hill NW3, Hampstead tube stop. Open pub hours.*

The French House. This wartime hangout of the French Resistance serves *vin ordinaire* and Pernod, has walls crammed with French pugilists, and a bar crammed with arty networkers.... *Tel 0171/437–2799. 49 Dean St. W1, Leicester Square tube stop. Open pub hours.*

LONDON ⌣ THE BAR SCENE

The George Inn. The ultimate Dickens inn. Though he drank nearly everywhere in town, this one really looks the part, with galleries and cobbled courtyard. It's been a pub since the 16th century—Shakespeare vintage, and they claim he performed here.... *Tel 0171/407–2056. 77 Borough High St. SE1, London Bridge tube stop. Open pub hours.*

The Good Mixer. An unreconstructed old-gits pub adopted by Indie music fans.... *Tel 0171/916–7929. 30 Inverness St. NW1, Camden Town tube stop. Open pub hours.*

The Gore Bar. This after-work club for chefs and restauranteurs has a dark and comfortable bar made for martinis.... *Tel 0171/581–5666. 190 Queensgate SW7, Gloucester Road tube stop. Open pub hours.*

Groucho. You can't get in unless you know a member, but this is so integral to the life of the London intelligentsia (drinking division) that it can't be left out.... *Tel 0171/439–4685. 44 Dean St. W1, Leicester Square tube stop. Open 9am–1am.*

Ground Floor. Found below the First Floor restaurant, this distressed-decor, vodka-shot-and-beer bar is one stop on the Notting Hill crawl.... *Tel 0171/243–8701. 186 Portobello Rd. W11, Ladbroke Grove tube stop. Open pub hours.*

The Holly Bush. Up a Hampstead back street is the pub you seek—cozy, nook-filled, open fireplaces, and nicotine-stained paintwork.... *Tel 0171/435–2892. 22 Holly Mount NW3, Hampstead tube stop. Open pub hours.*

The House. Sort of a wine bar; also a jazz hangout, with karaoke Mondays; and a so-so restaurant in a useful location.... *Tel 0171/435–8037. 34 Rosslyn Hill NW3, Hampstead tube stop. Open Mon–Fri 12pm–1am; Sat, Sun 10am–midnight.*

The Island Queen. A friendly sort of place with a good jukebox, good beer, giant caricature puppets on the ceiling, a pool table, and a mixed-age Islingtonian (half-granola, half-media) crowd.... *Tel 0171/359–4037. 87 Noel Rd. N1, Angel tube stop. Open pub hours.*

Jack Straw's Castle. This huge Hampstead landmark, named after the leader of the 1381 Peasant's Revolt, is now good only for the garden, where there are weekend barbecues in summer.... *Tel 0171/435 8885. North End Way NW3; Hampstead tube stop, then bus 210. Open pub hours.*

Kartouche. The gorgeous rich of Chelsea cruise each other in the bowels of this restaurant. Arrive before 9:30 to ensure entry and avoid cover. *Tel 0171/823–3515. 329–331 Fulham Rd. SW10, Fulham Broadway tube stop. Open Mon–Sat 6pm–midnight, Sun 6–11.*

The Lamb. A Dickens local. This is a pretty, all-round useful pub, slightly off the big tourist route, with summertime patio and standing-on-the-sidewalk drinking.... *Tel 0171/405–0713. 94 Lambs Conduit St. WC1, Holborn tube stop. Open pub hours.*

Le Shaker at Nam Long. High concept or what? This is a Vietnamese restaurant with a cocktail bar up front. It's a chat-up venue.... *Tel 0171/373–1926. 159 Old Brompton Rd. SW3, South Kensington tube stop. Open Mon–Sat 6:30–midnight.*

The Library. Despite posh high ceilings and grand windows, leather chesterfields, and oil paintings, there's no dress code for imbibing shots of "liquid history" in cognac form.... *Tel 0171/259-5599. Lanesborough Hotel, Hyde Park Corner SW1, Hyde Park Corner tube stop. Open pub hours.*

Living Room. Do here what you would in your own, except drink alcohol.... *Tel 0171/437–4827. 3 Bateman St. W1, Leicester Square tube stop. Open pub hours.*

The Lord Moon of the Mall. A fabulous space in the center of town, this was a major bank but is now a J. D. Wetherspoon pub. Salient characteristics: floorboards, no music, smoke-free zone, bargain Younger's Scotch Bitter.... *Tel 0171/ 839–7701. 16–18 Whitehall SW1, Charing Cross tube stop. Open pub hours.*

The Mayflower. From (near to) which the Pilgrims set sail for Plymouth Rock, this cute 18th-century, wood-beamed riverside pub retains permission to sell U.S. postage stamps.... *Tel 0171/237-4088. 117 Rotherhithe St. SW16, Rotherhithe tube stop. Open pub hours.*

Medicine Bar. They ripped out the old pub, slapped bright paint on the walls, and installed old couches; now all Islington drops by.... *Tel 0171/704–8056. 181 Upper St. N1, Angel tube stop. Open till midnight, pub hours Sun.*

Minogues. A rollicking Celtic time can be had in this Islington pub, with restaurant attached and appropriately Irish live music often.... *Tel 0171/354 4440. 80 Liverpool Rd. N1, Angel tube stop. Open pub hours.*

Mwah Mwah. The sound of a fashion-biz air kiss is the apt moniker of this Chelsea pub conversion with tartan-leop-ardskin chairs and a Beach Blanket Babylon (its young sis-ter) crowd.... *Tel 0171/823–3079. 241 Fulham Rd. SW3, Fulham Broadway tube stop. Open pub hours.*

O'Hanlons. Maybe the Kilburn Irish pubs are more authentic, but John O'Hanlon brews his own Irish ale, imports Guin-ness from Dublin, and serves it with his mother's soda bread, baked here daily.... *Tel 0171/837–4112. 18 Tysoe St. EC1, Farringdon tube stop. Open pub hours Mon–Fri.*

The Orange Brewery. The best microbrewery in town—some say the best pub, bar none. A Victorian house wraps around the cellar brew house, source of SW1, SW2, rich, dark Pimlico Porter, and seasonal specials.... *Tel 0171/730–5984. 37 Pimlico Rd. SW1, Sloane Square tube stop. Open pub hours.*

The Pharaoh and Firkin. Another Firkin pub, this one perhaps the biggest, with every weekend a sing-along 'round the old joanna (piano) bash, and Cam Ale on tap.... *Tel 0171/731–0732. 90 Fulham High St. SW6, Putney Bridge tube stop. Open pub hours.*

Po-Na-Na. Chelsea yuppies meet girlies to a house track in this self-styled souk basement bar, where it's a miracle the palms survive the nicotine cloud.... *Tel 0171/352–7127. 316 Fulham Rd. SW3, South Kensington tube stop. Open late.*

The Princess Louise. High Edwardian gorgeousness brought this beauty a preservation order, with a separate order for the gents.... *Tel 0171/405–8816. 208 High Holborn WC2, Holborn tube stop. Open pub hours.*

The Prospect of Whitby. In the early 16th century, this was a notorious haunt of cutthroats and wastrels that staged its own hangings. Now it's a well-known riverside tavern, with a sweet terrace.... *Tel 0171/481–1095. 57 Wapping Wall E1, Wapping tube stop. Open pub hours.*

The Raj. Distinguishing this pedestrian pub are its five hotly contested pool tables.... *Tel 0171/727–6332. 40 Holland Park Ave. W11, Holland Park tube stop. Open pub hours.*

Riki-Tik. Drop-dead cool bar, with chairs resembling space aliens upstairs and a steamy basement, with the requisite silly vodkas. No-suits policy had Quentin Tarantino barred.... *Tel 0171/437–1977. 23–24 Bateman St. W1, Leicester Sq. tube stop. Open 11am–1am Mon–Sat.*

The Ring. The real McCoy for students of the sweet science. Shoot the breeze about British boxing with publican and trainer Neville Axford.... *Tel 0171/928–2589. 72 Blackfriars Rd. SE1, Waterloo tube stop. Open pub hours.*

Rocky's. This peculiar chrome-clad, bilevel late bar has sports events broadcast on a big screen and no cover, so has surely been discovered by now.... *Tel 0171/287–1991. 3 New Burlington St. W1, Oxford Circus tube stop. Open 7pm–3am.*

The Royal Vauxhall Tavern. Just an old South London pub that happens to have hosted drag shows all its life.... *Tel 0171/ 582–0833. 372 Kennington Lane, SW8, Oval tube stop. Open pub hours.*

Shoeless Joe's. A swanky U.S.-style sports bar half-owned by England's tight-head prop (rugby, that's rugby). Upstairs are many monitors; down, a vast screen for the main event.... *Tel 0171/384–2333. 555 King's Rd. SW6, Fulham Broadway tube stop. Open pub hours.*

Soho House. Around the corner from Groucho, another members-and-guests-only Soho haunt of media types, though these are younger, less literary, more commercial, wearing shorter skirts.... *Tel 0171/734 5188. 40 Greek St. W1, Leicester Square tube stop. Open 9am–3am.*

The Spaniards Inn. Lovely trellised rose gardens get overrun with people in this 400-year-old pub, with blackened oak beams, Dick Turpin's guns (he drank here), and roaring open fires in winter.... *Tel 0171/455–3276. Spaniards Rd. NW3; Hampstead tube stop, then bus 210. Open pub hours.*

The Sports Café. The Canadians of Labatt's put this big bustling café/bar/restaurant here in the middle of the West End—it's mayhem, with 120 TV screens, DJs, and dance floor.... *Tel 0171/839–8300. 80 Haymarket SW1, Piccadilly Circus tube stop. Open Mon, Tue 12pm–1am; Wed, Thu till 2am; Fri, Sat till 3am; Sun till 11pm.*

The Sun. A place to do market research on British ale, real ale, in about 20 varieties on tap, no frills.... *Tel 0171/405–8278. 63 Lamb's Conduit St., Holborn tube stop. Open pub hours.*

Trader Vic's. Polynesian it ain't.... *Tel 0171/208–4113. Hilton, Park Lane W1, Hyde Park Corner tube stop. Open Mon–Sat 5:30pm–1am, Sun 7–11:30pm.*

The Village. A throbbing duplex Soho gay bar, about as cruisy as the West End gets.... *Tel 0171/434–2124. 81 Wardour St. W1, Piccadilly Circus tube stop. Open pub hours.*

Warwick Castle. Defiantly unpleasant to behold, this corner pub has been the center of Notting Hill life for at least a decade.... *Tel 0171/221–5140. 225 Portobello Rd. W11, Ladbroke Grove tube stop. Open pub hours.*

The Waterside. A hideaway off one of London's nastier streets, this barnlike pub has a terrace on the Battlebridge Basin, where people moor their canal barges and houseboats, and duckies bob about.... *Tel 0171/837–7118. 82 York Way N1, King's Cross tube stop. Open pub hours.*

Whisky Bar. Famous for 70 single malts, which you can try to drink in one night on "the Whisky Passport".... *Tel 0171/499–3464. 116 Piccadilly W1, Green Park tube stop. Open pub hours.*

The Windsor Castle. Not the Queen's country cottage, but a li'l old pub down Notting Hill with a sweet garden for summer and open fires for winter.... *Tel 0171/727–8491. 114 Campden Hill Rd. W11, Notting Hill Gate tube stop. Open pub hours.*

World's End. Major space for minors to mingle; not as trendy as they hope.... *Tel 0171/267–5086. 174 Camden High St. NW1, Camden Town tube stop. Open pub hours.*

The Yard. This gay-oriented Soho cafe/bar does, indeed, have a little courtyard for coffee or beer, as well as two floors of bars that buzz by night.... *Tel 0171/437–2652. 57 Rupert St. W1, Piccadilly Circus tube stop. Open pub hours.*

Ye Olde Cheshire Cheese. Ye original hokey tourist hostelry that's been open more than three centuries, with sawdust-strewn floors and great blackened beams.... *Tel 0171/ 353–6170. 145 Fleet St. EC4, Chancery Lane tube stop. Open pub hours.*

Ye Olde Swiss Cottage. This was a perfectly good hideous, unyuppied pub, but they blew it. Now it's neo-Victorian, but still worth a visit for the six-table pool club.... *Tel 0171/ 722–3487. 98 Finchley Rd. NW3, Swiss Cottage tube stop. Open pub hours.*

Central London Bars

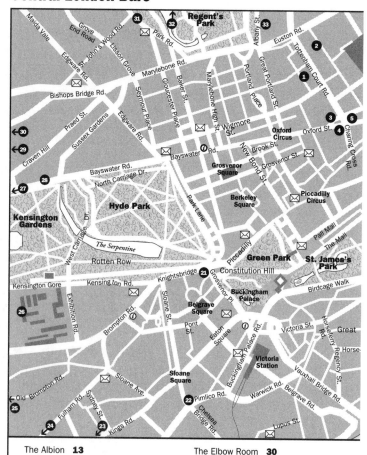

The Albion **13**
The American Bar **8**
Angel Café Bar **13**
babushka **18**
Beach Blanket Babylon **29**
The Black Cap **33**
Bradley's **3**
Break for the Border **4**
The Cittie of York **9**
The Columbia **28**
Come the Revolution **23**
Cottons Rhum Shop **33**
Cyberia Cyber Café **1**
The Devonshire Arms **33**
Drill Hall **2**

The Elbow Room **30**
First Out **5**
The Flask **32**
The Freemason's Arms **32**
The George Inn **17**
The Good Mixer **33**
The Gore Bar **26**
Ground Floor **29**
The Holly Bush **32**
The House **32**
The Island Queen **13**
Jack Straw's Castle **32**
Kartouche **24**
The Lamb **10**
Le Shaker at Nam Long **25**

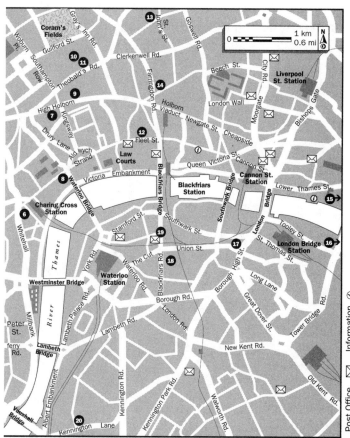

Post Office ⊠   Information ⓘ

Mayfair, St. James's & Piccadilly Bars

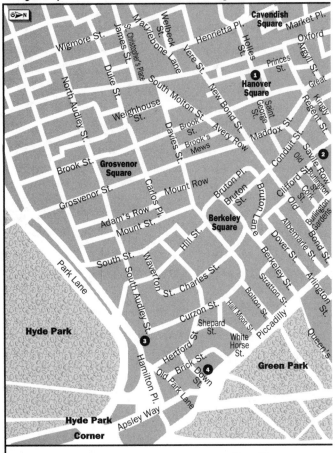

The Atlantic **6**
Bar Sol Ona **19**
Café Bohème **17**
Café Royal **7**
The Coach and Horses **18**

The Edge **13**
Flamingo **1**
The Flyman and Firkin **20**
Freedom Café Bar **10**
The French House **12**
Groucho **16**

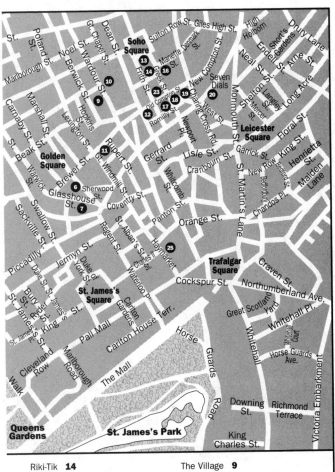

Riki-Tik **14**	The Village **9**
Rocky's **2**	Whisky Bar **4**
Soho House **23**	The Yard **11**
The Sports Café **25**	
Trader Vic's **3**	

the

arts

3

What London is most
famous for is, of course,
theater, and the scope and
bravery of the best theater
companies here is worthy
of any hype. The gamut
runs from the dozen or so

everlasting musicals such as *Cats* and *Phantom of the Opera*, about which we have nothing new to say, to the very newest in physical theater, which tends to come from elsewhere in Europe. Every touring company visits London sooner or later, so you end up with the best of all worlds: indigenous highbrow, Shakespeare, West End (London's Broadway), homegrown experimental, and imported avant-garde. Look out for the annual **London International Festival of Theatre (LIFT)** in June for concentrated doses of Catalan mimes and French nouvelle clowning. Crossover genres like physical theater (**Theatre de Complicité** are masters of this), new circus (look for **Ra Ra Zoo** and **Archaos**), narrative dance (**Yolanda Snaith, Bunty Matthias**), comedic performance (**Rose English**, for instance) are worth seeking out here if you're a true fan of living theater, and not just worshiping at the shrine of the traditional proscenium arch and three acts. Not that there's anything wrong with the **National Theatre**, and the **Royal Shakespeare Company**. Quite the opposite. If you've only time for one performance, something at the **Barbican** or **South Bank** is your safest bet (but check out the **Almeida, Royal Court** and **Lyric**, too). Pub theater's always been a London thing. It's exactly as it sounds, but you don't have to drink. Most pub theaters are in back or upstairs from the saloon, and tickets are about the price of a couple of pints.

Dance is more than healthy, too. The most pointes go to the **Royal Ballet**, but there's plenty of fresher choreographic events from home (Michael Clark's a Londoner) and abroad—much of it showcased in the monthlong **Dance Umbrella** in fall. The global love affair with opera hasn't passed London by, with the two major venues—the swanky **Royal Opera House**, and the **English National Opera's Coliseum**—joined by bursts of chorus at **Sadler's Wells** and **Holland Park**, and all over the place during the summertime **London Opera Festival**. Classical music listeners can scale down from the **London Symphony Orchestra** at the Barbican, or the **Royal Philharmonic** at the South Bank, to (often free) lunchtime recitals in churches. The big baton is **The Proms at the Albert Hall**, all summer long: nearly nightly concerts broadcast on national radio. The film scene features the usual Hollywood hits, six months after you've seen them, European productions that never got distribution in the U.S., and a fading selection of repertory theaters. Comedy thrives, however—this is the home of "Monty Python's Flying Circus" and "Absolutely Fabulous," after all.

Getting Tickets

The best way to get theater tickets is to go to the box office of the theater itself, or to call it with your plastic in hand. There's nothing wrong with ticket agents, like **First Call** (tel 0171/240–7941) or **Ticketmaster** (tel 0171/413–3321), unless you hate to pay the reasonable booking fee, and they do come up trumps for major rock gigs, or for when you're having a theater orgy and want to book several shows. If that's you, **Keith Prowse** can be called before you leave home, at the New York office (tel 212/398–1430 or 800/669–8687), as can **Edwards & Edwards** (tel 212/944–0290 or 800/223–6108); and **Ticketmaster** also has a U.S. 800 number (tel 800/775–2525). If you're planning a theater fest, are a control freak, and want to do it all yourself, send for the *Complete Guide to London's West End Theatres* (£9.95 plus p&h from the Society of London Theatre, tel 0171/836–0971; Bedford Chambers, The Piazza, Covent Garden, WC2E 8HQ), which has seating plans and booking information for all the West End houses. If you're cheap, broke, or smart, wait till you're in London, and line up at the indispensable **Half Price Ticket Booth** (no telephone) on the southwest corner of Leicester Square, which has tickets for performances later the same day at about 25 theaters (Monday–Saturday 2:30–6:30pm, from noon for matinees; cash only; £2 service charge). Hotels—including those with a dedicated theater desk—charge a larger fee than the phone bookers, and are only worth using if you're lazy, loaded, or longing to see Lloyd Webber's latest, in which case the best of them (the Savoy, the Athenaeum, the Dorchester…) may come up with the impossible, pricey ticket. Those shows, predictably, are the most likely to harbor a crop of **scalpers** outside (known as ticket touts here). Just say no. Never buy from a guy furtively brandishing a fistful of tickets—common sense will tell you when there's someone with a legitimate extra one. Every single theater keeps at least one row of **house seats** back till the last possible moment, for emergency oversales, and unexpected situations, plus a dozen or two **returns**. Policies on how these are dispensed vary, but be prepared to stand on line, possibly in the morning, probably an hour before curtain, with no guarantee of success. On the other hand, you may find yourself in the stalls (orchestra) at the Royal Opera House for a song (i.e., a £85+ seat for about £22). You'll see the term "concessions" a lot. These are senior citizens, students, people on the dole (welfare) or claiming unemployment benefit, and children. Obviously,

LONDON ⟋ THE ARTS

only the first two categories may include you, and you'll need proof to qualify for ticket discounts, so get your ISIC, kids (International Student Identity Card). See below for a rundown of which theater offers which deals.

If it's a big new show, you don't want to spend your vacation on line, and money's no object, check out the **classified ads** in the *Standard* for sort-of-legitimate scalpers who bought blocks of tickets and are off-loading them at a premium. But the toughest London ticket to acquire is this season's hottest fringe production (often called "Off–West End" in imitation of New York's "off-Broadway" appellation). Hotel dudes who use contacts to secure impossible West End high-price tickets can't swing the fringe, and the London theater buffs will have bought out the house by the time you catch the buzz. But be comforted: these are the shows that invariably transfer to the West End (anything by the brilliant **Theatre de Complicité**), or New York (*Hamlet*, starring Ralph Fiennes), and, if you're patient, will eventually become movies (*Les Liaisons Dangereuses*).

The Lowdown

The West End... Ah, the great London theatah. How fabulous, how famous, how intellectual... how very disappointing it can be. "West End" refers to the 50-odd mainstream houses, most of which are in that neighborhood—with a few exceptions, like the excellent **Royal Court** in Sloane Square, the very cute **Greenwich Theatre**, which makes a perfect end to the quintessential London Great Day Out, and the venerable, estimable **Old Vic**, which was reclaimed from the dead not too long ago, and now mounts many not-to-be-missed productions. The weird thing about West End is its ever-closer resemblance to New York's Broadway, with productions transferring back and forth across the Atlantic like so much stock from the Gap. To be fair, though, downright West End disappointment usually arises from a combo of overinflated expectations, a large dent in the pocketbook, and a bad pick. The London *Les Misérables* (nicknamed "The Glums" by some here) or any of the 53 Lloyd Webber monstrosities—sorry, monster hits—will please you as much as a high-school production of *Fiddler on the Roof,* if you hate musicals. Look for the houses that pitch their brow higher—like the **Theatre Royal Haymarket**, the **Aldwych**, the **Arts**, the **Cambridge**, the **Comedy**, the **Garrick**, and more.

And the nationals... The easiest, safest way to avoid disappointment when choosing a play is to select from the current season at the **National Theatre**, or **The Barbican**. The latter is where the **Royal Shakespeare Company (RSC)** resides for half the year. Many screen stars—from Ralph Fiennes to Patrick Stewart (Captain Picard!) earned their stripes on this legitimate stage, and an RSC production practically comes with a warranty. Nobody does the Bard better, though look to the Globe (not to be confused with the Shaftsbury Avenue Gielgud, which was The

Globe until 1994) for maximum authenticity, and else-where for the avant-garde interpretation. The **Barbican Theatre** holds nearly 700 people in the orchestra (here-after, we'll call the expensive seats by their English name: "the stalls"), and a further 475 on three tiers of circles—not the most comfortable of arrangements, perhaps, like the poor Barbican Centre itself which bounds it. The rhinoceros of London buildings, it's an ill-conceived, peculiar-looking, unapproachable, grey, thick-skinned creature, which continues to endure general ridicule. Its system of "levels" makes no sense at all, so it's impossible to navigate, plus its restaurants are execrable. The Pit, you might call it, and they did—at least that's what they called the 185-seater studio theater, more out of accuracy (it's a sub-basement) than mischief. The **South Bank Centre**'s Olivier or Lyttelton theaters are so much better off for location. Also, whatever's playing, if it made it to one of these national stages, has been vetted by as many dramaturges, critics, producers, directors, and quality controllers as a Hollywood epic, and will be a good bet. Less so the South Bank's "theatre-in-the-round" studio, the Cottesloe, where embarrassing juvenilia alternates with exciting edge-of-the-seat new talent, in the smallest by far (400 seats max) of the three stages. The Olivier has room for 1,160, and is the biggest, but, with its steeply banked fan-shaped auditorium, it actually feels more intimate than the 890-seater traditional proscenium-arched Lyttleton, where the stage is the part that slopes.

The cheap seats... A little more on spending a little less. All the West End theaters dispense with their unsold seats through the Half Price Ticket Booth (see "Getting Tickets," above), but many of them, including the dozen Stoll-Moss theaters (the **Gielgud**, **Her Majesty's**, the **Apollo Hammersmith**, the **Cambridge**, and all those with the 494 phone prefix), usually sell half-price seats from the box office half an hour before curtain-up—to concessions only. Disabled persons with their escorts can always get the best seats at half price at the Stoll-Moss houses and at the **Barbican**, at less than half price at the **Aldwych**, and at discounted rates at the **National**. The National also has standby seats for around £10 for those unqualified for other special prices, on sale two hours before curtain-up, while the RSC at the Barbican's same-day seats are £8, but call to ask how you get them these days. Students should call the **Midland Bank Student Theatreline** for the day's good deals. Under-29s can buy the **Stage Pass**, too, which provides discounts to theaters and all kinds of arts events across the U.K. Mondays are great days for shows. Several theaters slash rates on this day—the **Royal Court** and the **Lyric** Hammersmith had all Monday seats at £5 at press time, the **Young Vic** was doing them half price, while the **Hampstead** and the **Almeida** had reduced rates—also for Saturday matinees at the latter. At the **Tricycle**, Monday to Wednesday are half the price of Thursday to Saturday, though there are 20 same-day seats at £5 on Thursdays.

Historic houses... An added frisson is appended to a West End theatrical experience if you see it in one of London's historic theaters, and none of these venues is more historic than the **Theatre Royal Drury Lane**, which has been a theater since 1663, though not exactly in this form, since it's been burned to the ground three times (so far). That's one more time than the **Royal Opera House**, which first went up in 1732, then went up (in flames) in 1808 and 1856. Management (John Anderson, who had managed to lose two previous theaters to fire, but still got the job) attempted to defray the cost of the first rebuilding by hiking the ticket cost—a mistake that led to two entire months of vehement public protest in 1809, known to posterity as the Old Price Riots. Despite the relative youth of these two (1812 and 1858, respectively), they're both Grade I listed historic buildings, as is the **Theatre Royal Haymarket**, first built in 1721, though this gorgeous version was put up by Regency star architect John Nash in 1821, and has been much adorned since. Its neighbor, **Her Majesty's** was the original home of Herbert Beerbohm Tree's drama school which became the world famous RADA (Royal Academy of Dramatic Art), and had William Congreve as its first manager. The only London hotel with its own theater is the **Savoy**, where the Cameron Mackintosh of his day, Richard D'Oyly Carte, had his company debut all those Gilbert and Sullivan operettas we know so well. Across the Strand is the **Lyceum**, reopening in fall 1996 after eight years of dark, having survived since 1771, sometimes as a dance hall, and having hosted Gielgud's 1938 *Hamlet*. A related moment was Dame Edith Evans's definitive "A haand baaaaag?" in the 1939 *Importance of Being Earnest* at the **Gielgud;** the theater was named in honor of that thesp on his ninetieth birthday in 1994. When Sir John was 48, the world's longest-running play, *The Mousetrap,* opened. The who-done-it was then transferred (around the time of Gielgud's seventieth birthday) to **St. Martin's,** where the butler still does it every night for non-English-speaking Japanese convention attendees. More interesting recent theater history happened at the **Shaftsbury,** where Sarah Bernhardt took her final 1921 London bow, and *Hair* opened in 1969 to swing the sixties out; now the Who's *Tommy* has been re-reviving the seventies.

Haunted houses... No guidebook is allowed to omit London's phantoms of the opera, although it's possible that no guidebook writer has ever seen one. Predictably, most of them frequent the oldest theater, **Theatre Royal Drury Lane,** including the famous Man in Grey who prefers a matinee, and is a surer predictor of hits than any living drama critic. He likes the Upper Circle, while the clown's clown, Joseph Grimaldi, has only been spotted in the stalls, and Victorian comedian Dan Leno (Jay's great grandad, for all we know), stays in his dressing room—in its mirror, in fact. The **Garrick** has a ghost prompter, who feeds the wrong lines from the wrong corner, and an encouraging patter-on-the-back, who helps get rid of stage fright en route from the upstairs dressing room. In the alley outside the **Adelphi,** William Terriss still walks where rival actor Richard Archer Prince stabbed him to death in 1897, while the **Duke of York**'s first owner, Violet Melnotte, still hangs around in the circle bar and, every night at ten, slams a heavy iron door that no longer exists.

On the fringe... The Fringe is the collective noun for all the other theaters—about the same number again as the West End houses. It's where the exciting stuff is—where the much-vaunted British reverence for the stage is still at large. The best of those known nowadays as "Off–West End" do theater as it might have been in its pre-movie heyday—with passion, conviction, and infectious adoration of the medium. Those with the best track record for supplying chills of awe are the **Almeida,** the **Bush,** the little **Gate, Riverside Studios,** the **Donmar Warehouse** (actually West End, but nobody remembers), and the increasingly yummy **Young Vic**. The Almeida demands a trek north, but this place hardly ever misses—it's worth it. Others often worth traveling to include the **Theatre Royal Stratford East**, which is good and multicultural; the **BAC** (Battersea Arts Centre), the beauteous old music hall; the **Hackney Empire;** and the Kilburn **Tricycle**. The **Old Bull** and the **Watermans Arts Centres** are also good, but *so* far out of town, you'd need to be thoroughly grabbed by the production. The **Orange Tree** in Richmond, conversely, is equally far away, but can be combined with sightseeing (Ham, Marble Hill Houses, the Park, and so on). Ditto **Hampstead**. Don't overlook the **Royal Court Theatre Upstairs** or the **Lyric Studio**, which are the factory outlets of their West End (though neither is situated anywhere near the actual West End) selves, mounting works experimental, debut, or in-the-round, while the theater at the redoubtable **ICA** (Institute of Contemporary Arts) is exactly as it sounds—avant-garde, yet slightly *worthy*. Many is the pretentious show we've endured here in the name of art.

Far out on the fringe... With little fringe places, usually secreted above pubs, behind cafes, or way out in the sticks, you're on your own. Quality, degree of professionalism, amount of scenery, size of audience—everything is so utterly variable that generalization would be foolish and misleading. If they're good enough for long enough, they get sucked into the "Off–West End" list, like the Gate, the Bush and the Almeida's neighbor, the original pub theater, the **King's Head**, which continues its slightly irritating conceit of quoting the price of your round in £sd—that's pre-decimal pounds, shillings, and pence. Other pub joints that enjoy a good reputation are the Battersea **Latchmere** (in its Grace Theatre), the Chelsea **Man in the Moon**, the Islington **Old Red Lion**, all longstanding. We've also cried real tears and/or laughed till we were sick at the **Canal Café Theatre** (in lovely Little Venice—a plus), and the **DOC Theatre Club**, though this may have been serendipitous, and can in theory happen in any London fringe theater.

Far out... Oddities abound on the performance scene, and represent some of the most amusing things in London, especially in the summer festival and outdoor theater season. The best-known outdoor theater actually counts as

West End, and is so well known it doesn't belong in this category—the **Regent's Park Open Air Theatre**. More obscure, but gaining ground every year, especially now that the *Evening Standard* sponsors it, is the adorable **Holland Park Open Air Theatre**. In the outer boroughs you'll find events and atmospheres and audiences you'd never find in town, in arts centers which sustain entire microeconomies and pseudosocieties. Just south of the river, the Battersea Arts Centre, usually known as **BAC**, in the old Wandsworth Town Hall, has its own British Festival of Visual Theatre in fall, and lots of good shows year-round. The northern version is the **Old Bull Arts Centre**, which, being in Barnet, is barely in London, yet is accessible on the end of the awful Northern Line, while way west is wonderful **Watermans Arts Centre**, which is especially great for world music and obscure, yet powerful, foreign drama in translation—all very cutting edge. If you want the hippest theater, forget West End, think East End. Here are the **Hackney Empire**—a fab palatial Edwardian music hall whose shows often hop between comedy, circus, dance, drama, and music in a hybrid horribly dubbed "New Variety"—and the most effortlessly PC of the big fringe theaters (but don't let that put you off), the **Theatre Royal Stratford East**. Even more correctly, the nearby **Tom Allen Arts Centre** does drumming workshops for gay youth groups and is very multicultural—the exact opposite, in fact, of the no-brain, fun-night-out **Brick Lane Music Hall** and its old-time cabaret dinner show. Back up north, at **Jackson's Lane**, you can get onstage yourself in various informal classes and workshops, many of them movement-oriented, and there's full awareness of other cultures here, too. The **Diorama**, on the edge of Regent's Park, is worth checking out for the place itself. It was a prototype cinema—images painted on glass revolved in the dome and were "projected" by natural light—then a rather scary hydrotherapy center early this century, and now approximates the atmosphere of a disused institution for the criminally insane. Its recent history has been a catalogue of demolition threats, so catch it while you can. Another roundhouse much threatened with extinction is the **Camden Roundhouse**, which was a groovy theater in the sixties, then a legendary punk venue in the seventies. Though built to rotate Industrial Revolution steam engines at the end of the line, you'd think it had been designed for its current use—to host visiting circuses. It looks like the Palais d'Hiver in Paris. Sort of related is a former power station on the fringes of the city, which is now the nerve center of British circus arts, known as **The Circus Space**. Performances are limited in number and mixed in success, but stirring, sometimes transcendent; and if you're in town long enough, take enough Circus Space classes, and train hard enough, you can be in the show.

Starring who? Where?... Don't assume that the stars frequent only the big West End houses. Also don't assume that what counts as a star here will mean anything at all to you. We have our own trash TV, you know, and its denizens like to break out and tread the boards occasionally—superstars like Shane Richie and Lily Savage. Conversely, there are British stage actors who broke out of the proscenium arch and find it hard to get back very often—like Emma Thompson and her former spouse, Kenneth Branagh; Ralph Fiennes; Sir Anthony Hopkins; and, yes, old baldy, Patrick Stewart. The real stars of the British stage, though, are the actors who are dedicated to it, and not concerned with celluloid fame. Some got that anyway, yet continue to adore the London stage—like supernovas of the genre, the great Dames Maggie Smith, Diana Rigg, and Judi Dench—while others take the odd movie role, but manage to remain obscure in America while being household names at home—like Michael Gambon, Julia McKenzie, and Richard Briers. You'll also find the younger generation of Brit thespians who appear in Merchant Ivory productions (James Wilby, Rufus Sewell, Rupert Graves) and make regular West End and **National Theatre** appearances; and then there are the Great Actors whose fame you'll have to get translated by your London friends: Fiona Shaw, Janet McTeer, and Geraldine McKewan are making tidal waves on the London stage, for instance. Now, you would have thought that the West End would be the only place to see such large talents, but you'd be wrong. The **Almeida**, the **Bush**, and the **Young Vic** continue to attract more than their fair share of giant stars, right up to and including actors with the last name Redgrave.

The dance... This city's up there with the best, in both classical and young choreographer departments. The ballet is biggest and most glossy when given by The Royal Ballet at the **Royal Opera House**. Stars they claim as their own include Irek Mikhamedov and Darcey Bussell, but visiting feet dance here, too, as they do at the other big ballet place, **Sadler's Wells**, where there's also flamenco and tango and specialist dancers are always dropping by. Famous former Royal Ballet members include Wayne Sleep, who has his own TV specials, and his diametric opposite, the beautiful bad boy Michael Clark. The **English National Ballet**, being a touring company, isn't always around, but does stop twice a year, in summer, at the **Coliseum** and **Royal Festival Hall**, which it revisits at year's end to do the *Nutcracker* thing, and then the *Swan Lake* thing in the new year. The smaller South Bank auditorium, the **Queen Elizabeth Hall**, also hosts big-name and up-and-coming dance companies. In 1995, an unprecedented dance phenomenon hit town, in the unlikely setting of the **Apollo Hammersmith**—a kind of marathon mass Irish jig called Riverdance, which proved so popular, we wouldn't be surprised if it's still around somewhere.

The modern dance... If your taste is more Clark than Sleep, **The Place** is your place, with a 300-seat theater designed specially for dance, plus classes (see Sports), and much visiting by multicultural troops; the **Lilian Baylis Theatre**, **Riverside Studios**, and the **ICA** also favor modern programs. For all kinds of ethnic dance and fusion—martial arts, South Asian dance theater, and western choreography to a hip-hop DJ, for instance—go to **Jacksons Lane**. While if you want to experience eurhythmy, the **Rudolph Steiner Theatre** is not just the only place in town, but one of the only ones in the world. At the East End **Chisenhale Dance Space** there are programs of new work, new choreography, new everything. To see still further into the state of the art, look out for the excellent London dance festivals, like the top-dog summer or fall **Dance Umbrella**, which unites dancers from all over the world; the springtime Spring Loaded, and the Islington Dance Festival. Some homegrown names to catch include Yolanda Snaith, Bunty Matthias, the Richard Alston Company, and Lea Anderson's Featherstonehaughs (pronounced "Fanshawes"—a troop of guys in boots and suits).

Verdi to Schnittke... As it seems to be everyplace these days, opera is big in London. A first night at the **Royal Opera House** is one hot ticket, especially when Jonathan Miller (doctor-director-sixties satirist-TV presenter-renaissance man) has a new production, or one of the divas is in town. London has preferred tenors, ever since the aria "Nessun Dorma" from *Turandot* was the 1990 World Cup (soccer) theme tune, and Pavarotti was blasting out from every pub jukebox. Every bit as good as the Royal Opera is the English National Opera, which lives at the **Coliseum**, off Trafalgar Square. The main differences are that the ENO costs less to see, and sings in English. The Royal Opera gets more of the ultimate stars, and projects "surtitles" over the stage, just like the New York City Opera. The ENO is far more likely to mount Glass or Schnittke, while the House will be first with your Wagner. Another theater with an opera program is the Islington **Sadler's Wells**, which is where to find the D'Oyly Carte Company, founded by Richard D'Oyly Carte, partly for producing the Englishissimo Gilbert and Sullivan. It still churns out *The Yeomen of the Guard, The Pirates of Penzance,* etc., as well as other people's operettas. **South Bank Centre**'s three auditoria, as well as the **Barbican**, all mount the occasional semi-staged performance, and recitals, too. If the music is not your top priority, then don't pass up the **Holland Park Open Air Theatre**, wherein little companies stage full-scale productions of *La Traviata* and *Tosca*—and *The Yeomen of the Guard*—accompanied by the bedtime screeches of resident peacocks, and a Technicolor sunset. A big event is the summertime London Opera Festival, including at least one performance beamed direct from the Royal Opera House stage onto giant screens in the **Covent Garden Piazza**—at no charge.

Mozart to Martinu... The classical music scene is a thriving, throbbing cornucopia of everything from Bach masses to percussion concerti. Indigenous world-famous orchestras and ensembles include the Royal Philharmonic Orchestra—which plays at home in the **Royal Festival Hall**—and the less glam London Symphony Orchestra, which lives at the **Barbican** with the English Chamber Orchestra. You'll find a lot of Henry Purcell and Thomas Tallis around—not just because they're English, but because Baroque is in vogue, and it was Purcell's 300th birthday in 1995. Look out for the Tallis Scholars, and the exquisite Early Music vocal group The Sixteen; The King's Singers are a famous British a cappella ensemble with an eclectic repertoire. Appreciated modern maestri include performer/composer Michael Nyman, of *The Piano* and Peter Greenaway movies fame, and the amazing deaf percussionist Evelyn Glennie—both ubiquitous. As for venues… a lot goes on in a few places. Between them, the **South Bank Centre** and the **Barbican** have most of the major recitals and concerts sewn up, the former with its Russian doll set of three halls of diminishing size—the **Royal Festival** and **Queen Elizabeth Halls**, and the **Purcell Room**. Other than these, there's the glorious **Wigmore Hall** behind Oxford Street, and the blowsy Victorian **Albert Hall**, which is most remarkable for the wonderful summer series of Henry Wood Promenade Concerts, or Proms. Often neglected, because nobody knows quite how to get there, is the newest hall of all, the Canary Wharf **Cabot Hall**, which has world-music-type, as well as classical, sounds. Better for a gentle evening out is a recital at one of these two historic houses: Holland Park's **Leighton House** and Hampstead's **Burgh House**, while one of the best things to do with a summer's evening is to head out **Kenwood** way, to the concert bowl there, especially when they're doing the *1812 Overture* or *Music For the Royal Fireworks,* both of which come complete with pyrotechnics. Set out early and bring a picnic—if the weather's smiling, these events are mobbed. The four London conservatoires— the **Royal Academy of Music**, Trinity College, Guildhall, and the **Royal College of Music**—do put their students on the stage, both in their own concert halls and abroad in London.

Pew music… Some of the major classical music venues, and certainly the most numerous, are churches. A few, like the leader of the pack, **St. John's Smith Square**, are deconsecrated; others, including the other big cheese, **St. Martin-in-the-Fields**, retain their pasture, and operate a double life as house of entertainment/house of God. The latter spawned the famous baroque ensemble the Academy of St. Martin-in-the-Fields, by the way. Others of the genre include several Wren City churches, like **St. Giles in the Barbican**, and **St. James's Garlickhythe**, plus the Piccadilly Wren with the plastic spire (O.K., fiberglass), St. James's **Southwark Cathedral** is a major venue, and look out for the program at Nicholas Hawkesmoor's **Christ Church Spitalfields**, because the building's as glorious as the music. A trio of churches better known for society weddings, which throw the odd musical soirée, are **St. George's Hanover Square**, **St. Margaret's Westminster**, and **St. Peter's Eaton Square**, the latter with a fine organ, which comes in handy. However, the grandest and most gorgeous church venue of all is that breathtaking center of London, **Westminster Abbey**, whose services are not, of course, concerts, but whose concerts are worth traveling far for. Concerts in churches, by the way, are big bargains—and often they're entirely free, especially at lunchtime.

In concert... Most jazz, blues, and world music places qualify as nightclubs, and are therefore to be found in the Clubs chapter. However, a few places should be mentioned in this context as sit-down venues for big bands—as in the Big Band Sound of the forties and as in the Art Ensemble of Chicago—and that stratum of serious musician big name that includes, say, Cleo Laine, Carla Bley, Pat Metheny, Tito Puente, plus the likes of Paul Simon and Eric Clapton, whose followers are on the mature side.... Between them the **Queen Elizabeth Hall**, the little **Purcell Room**, and the **Albert Hall** have this side of the music spectrum pretty much covered, though the giant stadia at **Wembley** should be mentioned in this context for the very biggest cheeses, and also **Cabot Hall**. Other sit-down venues for less frenetic concert attendance are the ambiance-challenged **Apollo Hammersmith**, and the very lovely **Hackney Empire**, both proscenium-arched, raked auditorium theaters, and the outlying (but worth the cab outlay) **Vortex**—a civilized cabaret-style way to take in the avant-garde side of the jazz repertoire. Maybe the **Union Chapel** deserves to be mentioned here, as well as in Clubs, since it was a church—it's a smallish place for biggish names.

Cinema... This is what a movie theater is called, without the merest hint of snobbishness, and a movie is called a film, so get used to it. The movie scene in London has been sadly diminished since the closure of two of its best-loved, longest-running repertory houses, the Scala, and the Electric (the latter may have reopened, though probably not as a rep theater). Still, what's left in the hardcore cinephile's domain isn't bad, and it stars the amazing **National Film Theatre (NFT)** in the South Bank Centre, where two houses, plus a screen at the Museum of the Moving Image, bring what has to be the world's widest-ranging programming to London. Wait long enough and it turns up here. This is also the nerve center of the November **London Film Festival**, which also goes on in Leicester Square. The other central London rep house is the **ICA Cinematheque**, which limits itself to pretentious movies. Catch Powell & Pressburger's *Peeping Tom* at the Hampstead **Everyman**, and you get the frisson of having the actual cinema you're in mentioned on screen. Not only is it the world's first repertory cinema (dating from 1933), but it's one of the most lovable, from its four different movies a day to its oatcakes and coffee to its picturesque location. The aforementioned are all cinema clubs, so you have to buy membership, from 40p to £1.50/day, unlike at the remaining three reps—the Brixton **Ritzy** (south), Hackney **Rio** (east) and Hammersmith **Riverside** (west). Observe the embryonic stages of local celluloid in Camden at the **London Film-Makers' Co-op**, a sixties relic that survived to screen shorts in minimal comfort, and brings on the next generation of directors competing for the ten places at the National Film School and the miniscule annual British Film Institute budget.

The movies... The biggest first-run screens in town are clustered together in Leicester Square. The **Warner West End** is the multiplexiest of all, with nine screens (numbers 5 and 7 are biggest), but the **Odeon Marble Arch** has the largest screen and auditorium (seats for 1,262) in town—it's a shame it only shows the latest Schwarzenegger vehicle. Anyway, why bother with Hollywood flicks you could have seen at home weeks ago? London's best movie moments (apart from repertory) are available at the art houses. The swankiest salon this side of the DreamWorks private screening room is the aptly named Knightsbridge **Minema**, where the 68 seats are vast armchairs, and Michael Jordan could stretch his legs. In the West End, it's a toss-up between the **Lumière** and the **Curzon** for which is the pleasantest, plushest, poshest place to view high-caliber world cinema, though the **Prince Charles** is definitely the cheapest, showing the same films, but months later for a couple of quid. The hippest houses with consistently good movies are the three **Screens**: **On the Hill**, **On the Green**, and **On Baker Street**, while the least hip, but most fun movie house of all is **UCI Whiteleys**—a big night out at a multiplex, where the Pick 'n' Mix candy counter is bigger than the average screen, and there's a real late-opening mall wrapped around the eight theaters, to make teens feel at home.

Fiestas... The year's arts festival calendar starts with the relatively new **London Arts Season**, which is the packaging of whatever's going on anyway, with a special phone number and information center for multiple booking. It's a good thing, because it cheers up the horrible months of February and March. The aforementioned **London Film Festival** is on a par with those in New York and Venice, and may represent your only chance to gauge the state of Egyptian, Norwegian, and Welsh cinema. Among the new work you'll find screenings of cults, greats, and obscure classics, and—disconcertingly—major U.S. releases which haven't come out in England yet. The NFT also hosts two minority fests, the Lesbian & Gay Film Festival in early spring, and the October Jewish Film Festival, plus a July weekend for sci-fi geeks, called Fantasm. The year's biggest theater date is the roughly monthlong, summertime **LIFT—the London International Festival of Theatre**—in which the fringe venues of the city are divided by the maximum number of contemporary, outrageous, famous, and obscure experimental companies from literally all over the world, working in all disciplines, in all languages. Sometime after that (it's difficult to be precise here, since these things change year on year; some years have even been bereft of LIFT), **Alternative Arts**—an administrative body that lays on events in all media, from new artists' installations in empty shops to full-scale operas—mounts a summer season at Victoria Embankment Gardens. Check the listings. The fall **Dance Umbrella** covers the spectrum, as its name suggests—Merce Cunningham came by last year, and there are always supporting workshops and screenings and such, with the bulk of events at The Place and the ICA. Musical fests are concentrated in summer, from the season at **Kenwood** to the most-famous Proms, or the BBC

Henry Wood Promenade Concerts. For the past hundred years, from July to September, there's been a big-deal, mostly classical, though sometimes jazz, gig every night at **Albert Hall**, culminating in the Last Night of the Proms, in which student types in college scarves roar "Land of Hope and Glory," giggle, and throw streamers. The name refers to the bargain promenade—standing, roaming about, sitting on the floor—tickets. Before the Proms, look out for the London Opera Festival and the (late June) **City of London Festival**, with chamber music, outdoor theater, jazz ensembles, and poetry readings and such secreted all over the square mile, from church to piazza. Two local riverside arts fests are the early June **Greenwich Festival**, downstream, and the mid-July **Richmond Festival**, upstream, both with a full deck of all the arts. Then, in early September, festivities erupt all over the river, in the newish **London Thames Festival** that's mostly fireworks and parades. Nothing but parades—with soca, calypso, reggae, ragga, sound systems bigger than houses, goat curry and Red Stripe beer—is the August Bank Holiday **Notting Hill Carnival**, and who cares if it's art.

Reading aloud... Considering Britain's literary heritage, you'd think there'd be a book event four times a day, and it is indeed a growth area in the nightlife department, though you still have to look under things and behind things to find the writer. Of the bookstores that host meet-the-author readings, **Dillons**, **Waterstones**, **Hatchards**, and **Books Etc.** are the most likely to do evenings, sometimes with hors d'oeuvres (especially at Waterstones). More modern are poetry slams-cum-open-mike performance nights, like Apples and Snakes every other week at **BAC**, the twice-weekly **Pull My Daisy** at Madame Jo Jo's and Mas Café, and the long-running Tuesday night **Brixton Poets** get-together at a park in Brixton. The most formal, highest-ticket (setting you back at least £4) spoken-word events are at the South Bank, at the **Royal Festival Hall's** Voice Box, from which you can repair to the Poetry Library and listen further to recordings, and at the **National Theatre's** Platforms series, in which artists are also invited to speak about their work. Call the **Poetry Society** for the latest readings information—if you dare. It's terribly insidery.

Ha ha ha ha... The same entertainment trend that popularized opera has rendered formerly fashionable **comedy**—especially stand-up—a bit less groovy, but so-o ubiquitous. You can catch the funny guys at tons of places, including the spot that kicked off the thing called "alternative comedy", the London equivalent of "Saturday Night Live" that spawned various cult performers who became the mainstream in the eighties (and still are): **The Comedy Store**. It's in a posher place than the old dive, but still reliably purveys a laugh. Of the many places with "comedy" in the name, pick the **Comedy Café**, which was purposely built for comedy, as was the Camden **Jongleurs**, part of the ever-expanding Dingwalls city in Camden Lock, and the sister of the very popular **Jongleurs Battersea**. At all of these laugh factories, it's wise to book in advance. The **Canal Café Theatre**'s useful for its late revues, and picturesquely located (although a bit far from the tube). The **Hackney Empire** does a lot of comedy, including the Monday regular **Smiley's Cut Price Comedy Club** ("for the cheapest laughs in town"), which features some pretty big names. Who are the big names? If you ever catch "Whose Line Is It Anyway?," you'll know Josie Lawrence, Paul Merton, Jim Sweeney, John Sessions, Tony Slattery, and their fellow five-star improvisers, who all appear on stage more or less regularly. A rare but regular performer who never has, and says he never will, appear on TV is Eddie Izzard, who sometimes wears women's clothes, and who's supposed to be the funniest guy in the world.

Small pleasures... Entertainment for very young people includes several children's theaters, as you'd expect in the world's theater capital. The oldest is the **Unicorn**, here since WWII, serving up puppets and new plays and workshops, and the **Little Angel** is also no youngster, at about 30 years old. The **Movingstage Marionette Company** lives up to its name by floating on a barge on Regent's Canal. The only kid's theater actually built as a kid's theater is the **Polka Children's Theatre**, which has won awards, despite its being way out in Wimbledon. The trouble with children's theater, however, is that it only deals in matinees. The only late-night fun for kids is at **Pippa Pop-ins**, the hotel for under-twelves.

The Index

Adelphi. A West End theater since the beginning of the last century, though this version dates from the thirties.... *Tel 0171/344–0055 (credit card bookings). 411–412 Strand WC2, Covent Garden tube stop.*

Albert Hall. The jolly, red, round, domed concert hall opposite the Hyde Park memorial to Victoria's beloved consort, Albert, looks like a birthday cake designed by Josiah Wedgwood, holds 8,000 people, and has not the best acoustics in the land, but is nevertheless home to the Proms.... *Tel 0171/589–3203. Kensington Gore SW7, South Kensington tube stop.*

Aldwych. A West End theater. Stoppard is on at press time.... *Tel 0171/416–6003. The Aldwych WC2, Covent Garden tube stop.*

Almeida. Possibly London's best Off–West End theater is always exciting, once you've tracked it down.... *Tel 0171/359–4404. Almeida St. N1, Angel tube stop.*

Alternative Arts. An operation that produces free events of all sorts, including a summer festival at Victoria Embankment Gardens.... *Tel 0171/375–0441.*

Apollo Hammersmith. Major concert and big-event venue without much soul, but plenty of space, sometimes listed under its sponsor's name ("Labatt's Apollo"). It's a sit-down place.... *Tel 0181/741–4868. Queen Caroline St. W6, Hammersmith tube stop.*

Artsline. A telephone information service giving access information for the disabled.... *Tel 0171/379–8900.*

Arts Theatre. A West End theater.... *Tel 0171/836–2132. 6–7 Great Newport St. WC2, Leicester Square tube stop.*

The Barbican. The major arts center's two theaters are home to the RSC; its auditorium home to the London Symphony Orchestra.... *Tel 0171/638–8891; 24-hour info: music 0171/638–4141, RSC 0171/628–2295. Silk St. EC2, Barbican/ Moorgate tube stop.*

BAC. A.k.a. the Battersea Arts Centre—a long way out, but often worth it for a variety of arts.... *Tel 0171/223–2223. 176 Lavender Hill SW11, Clapham Junction BR.*

Books Etc. Bookstore with cafe and readings.... *Tel 0171/ 379–6838. 120 Charing Cross Rd. WC2, Tottenham Court Road tube stop.*

Brick Lane Music Hall. An old-time cabaret dinner show in the Edwardian working-class tradition.... *Tel 0171/377–8787. 152 Brick Lane E1, Aldgate East tube stop. Closed Sun–Wed.*

Brixton Poets. A longstanding weekly (Tuesdays) gathering of southerly wordsmiths, more of a slam than a declamation.... *Tel 0181/567–1409. Prince Albert, Coldharbour Lane SW2, Brixton tube stop.*

Burgh House. An elegant Hampstead chamber music venue.... *Tel 0171/431–0144. New End Square NW3, Hampstead tube stop.*

Bush. Off–West End venue with sometimes controversial tastes.... *Tel 0181/743–3388. Shepherds Bush Green W12, Goldhawk Road tube stop.*

Cabot Hall. Canary Wharf is a North American business district stuck on the end of Camden, and this is its concert hall.... *Tel 0171/418–2783. Cabot Place West E14, Canary Wharf, Isle of Dogs, Docklands Light Railway.*

Cambridge. A West End theater.... *Tel 0171/494–5080. Earlham St. WC2, Covent Garden tube stop.*

Camden Roundhouse. A former train-shunting facility, hippie and punk landmark (in reverse order) now houses visiting

LONDON & THE ARTS

circuses of every ilk.... *Tel 0171/482–7318. Chalk Farm Rd. NW1, Chalk Farm tube stop.*

Canal Café Theatre. Its Little Venice waterside location is a bonus; there's a late cabaret after the play.... *Tel 0171/ 289–6054. Bridge House, Delamere Terrace W2, Warwick Avenue tube stop.*

Chisenhale Dance Space. An intimate East End venue specially designed to showcase new dance, with workshops, too.... *Tel 0181/981–6617. 64—84 Chisenhale Rd. E3, Mile End tube stop.*

Christ Church Spitalfields. Nicholas Hawkesmoor's church is being renovated, but still gives concerts.... *Tel 0171/377– 0287. Commercial St. E1, Spitalfields tube stop.*

Circus Space. Wherein nouveau circus is born and displayed— and the intrepid with time to spare can learn the ropes.... *Tel 0171/613–4141. Coronet St. N1, Old Street tube stop.*

City of London Festival. All over the City—meaning the Square Mile, the financial district, not the entire capital— there are concerts and performances and readings in indoor and outdoor settings for three weeks in early summer, starting late June.... *Tel 0171/248–4260.*

Coliseum. Home of the English National Opera.... *Tel 0171/ 632–8300; credit card reservations 0171/240–5258. St. Martin's Lane WC2, Charing Cross tube stop.*

Comedy Café. A city club with a varied program—and times. Call for the latest.... *Tel 0171/739–5706. 66 Rivington St. EC2, Old Street tube stop.*

Comedy Store. The first—and if not the best, at least one of the most reliable—of funny clubs.... *Tel 01426/914433 (info), 0171/344–4444 (credit card res.). Haymarket House, Oxendon St. SW1. Piccadilly Circus tube stop.*

Comedy Theatre. A West End theater.... *Tel 0171/369–1731. Panton St. SW1, Piccadilly Circus tube stop.*

Covent Garden Piazza. Here's the screen onto which opera is beamed during the London Opera Festival; here are classical buskers, too.... *Covent Garden, Covent Garden tube stop.*

Curzon. Very posh, as movie theaters go, this Mayfair art house tends to favor the French.... *Tel 0171/369–1720. Curzon St. W1, Green Park tube stop.*

Dance Umbrella. Covers contemporary dance from the most famous to the brand-new in a monthlong fall festival all over town, but based at The Place.... *Tel 0181/741–5881.*

Dillons. Bookstore, with readings.... *Tel 0171/636–1577. 82 Gower St. WC1, Goodge Street tube stop.*

Diorama. An eccentric yet glorious domed building on the edge of Regents Park, hosting all manner of arts events, fringe theater, and the occasional club night.... *Tel 0171/419–2000. 34 Osnaburgh St. NW1, Great Portland Street tube stop.*

DOC Theatre Club. Above a North London pub, this sometimes great fringe group plays—often Ibsen.... *Tel 0171/485–4303. Duke of Cambridge, 64 Lawford Rd. NW5, Kentish Town tube stop.*

Donmar Warehouse. Is it West End? Is it Off? Is it fringe? Cabaret? Who cares—this central place nearly always has something good on.... *Tel 0171/369–1732. Thomas Neal's, Earlham St. WC2, Covent Garden tube stop.*

Duke of York. A West End theater with a ghost and often interesting productions.... *Tel 0171/836–5122. St. Martin's Lane WC2, Leicester Square tube stop.*

Everyman. The world's first repertory cinema isn't in Hollywood, but in picturesque Hampstead. Great programming with up to four different films a day, and a cafe beneath. Membership costs 60p/year.... *Tel 0171/435–1525. Hollybush Vale NW3, Hampstead tube stop.*

Garrick. A West End theater.... *Tel 0171/494–5085. Charing Cross Rd. WC2, Leicester Square tube stop.*

Gate. This tiny, ambitious and well-known theater's been around forever.... *Tel 0171/229–0706. 11 Pembridge Rd. W11, Notting Hill Gate tube stop.*

Gielgud. West End theater named after that beloved thespian knight.... *Tel 0171/494–5065. Shaftsbury Ave. W1V, Piccadilly Circus tube stop.*

Greenwich Festival. For two weeks in early June (probably), the neighborhood of the Prime Meridian, from which the world's time is measured, bursts forth in music and dance.... *Tel 0181/317–8687.*

Greenwich Theatre. A West End theater, far from the West End.... *Tel 0181/858–7755. Crooms Hill SE10, Greenwich BR.*

Hackney Empire. A loverly old theater in the East End, where a lot of comedy happens—also plays and music.... *Tel 0181/985–2424. 291 Mare St. E8, Hackney Central BR.*

Hampstead Theatre. A serious Off–West End place that attracts the occasional big name.... *Tel 0171/722–9301. Avenue Rd. NW3, Swiss Cottage tube stop.*

Hatchards. Bookstore, with readings.... *Tel 0171/439–9921. 187 Piccadilly W1, Green Park tube stop.*

Her Majesty's. A gorgeous Victorian of a West End theater, in which Handel tried to get Londoners keen on opera, but in which Lloyd Webber is having more success with mass bookings for *Phantom*.... *Tel 0171/494–5400. Haymarket SW1, Piccadilly Circus tube stop.*

Holland Park Open Air Theatre. The cutest stage in town is in the ruins of a Jacobean mansion.... *Tel 0171/602–7856. Holland Park W8, Holland Park tube stop. Apr–Sept.*

ICA. The theater at the Institute of Contemporary Arts stages performance pieces, lectures, dance, and bizarre hybrids of same; the Cinemathèque favors obscure and artsy-fartsy films.... *Tel 0171/930–3647. The Mall SW1, Charing Cross tube stop.*

Jacksons Lane. A place in the north for dance, usually non-indigenous, with a community feel.... *Tel 0181/340–5226. Jackson's Lane N6, Highgate tube stop.*

Jongleurs. If you like the seething teenage tornado of Camden Lock, you'll laugh at the funny guys here.... *Tel 0171/924–2766. Dingwalls Building, Middle Yard, Camden Lock NW1, Chalk Farm tube stop.*

Jongleurs Battersea. One of the most popular comedy destinations in the capital, so reserve a table, especially on big-ger-name weekends.... *Tel 0171/924–2766. The Cornet, 49 Lavender Gardens SW11, Clapham Junction BR.*

Kenwood. The *sine qua non* of summer evening pastimes is a concert in the bowl across the lake.... *Tel 0181/348–6684. Hampstead Heath, Hampstead tube stop.*

King's Head. A very longstanding pub theater; at this one you can drink during the play, as long as you can figure out how much your pre-1972 £sd pint costs.... *Tel 0171/226–1916. 115 Upper St. N1, Highbury & Islington/Angel tube stop.*

Latchmere. Above a Battersea pub is this very good fringe theater, called the Grace.... *Tel 0171/228–2620. 503 Battersea Park Rd. SW11, Clapham Junction BR.*

Leighton House. Hear chamber music in Victorian splendor.... *Tel 0171/602–3316. 12 Holland Park Rd. W14, Kensington High Street tube stop.*

Lilian Baylis Theatre. A dance specialist in Islington.... *Tel 0171/713–6000. Arlington Way EC1, Angel tube stop.*

Little Angel. This longstanding children's theater eschews live actors for marionettes.... *Tel 0171/226–1787. 14 Dagmar Passage, Cross St. N1, Angel tube stop.*

London Arts Season. Two months of the city's arts offerings, packaged up and tied with a pretty ribbon, because it's February and March and nobody would go out otherwise. You can make multiple reservations at this number; ask about deals and special events.... *Tel 0171/839–6181 (Feb–Mar only). London Arts Information Centre, British Travel Centre, 12 Regent St. SW1, Piccadilly Circus tube stop.*

London Film Festival. The big event in the film year is a tub of stuff you saw at home last year, stuff from countries you didn't know had a movie industry, stuff from here that you'll see at home next year, and world cinema at its best. Screenings are at the NFT, the ICA and Leicester Square.... *Tel 0171/928–3232; 0171/633–0274 (recorded daily update). FIlm on the Square ticket and information booth, Leicester Square during festival. Early Nov.*

London Film-Makers' Co-op. Where to discover what's coming next in Brit movies, or in political-social issues, anyway. Screenings aren't luxurious, but the Engineer pub (see Late Night Dining) is across the street. A new lease on life begins in late 1996, when the co-op moves to Hoxton Square.... *Tel 0171/ 586–8516. 42 Gloucester Ave. NW1, Camden Town tube stop.*

London International Festival of Theatre (LIFT). Great new stuff from all over, at many locations, for a month in summer—usually starting mid-June.... *Tel 0171/490–9964.*

London Thames Festival. Not much to do with the arts, unless you count fireworks, sports, and parades, this new festival happens along the length of the river in early September.

Lumiere. A comfortable and rather elegant first-run art-house movie theater in the heart of theatreland.... *Tel 0171/379–3014. St. Martin's Lane WC2, Charing Cross tube stop.*

Lyceum. Reopening fall 1996.... *Strand WC2, Charing Cross tube stop.*

Lyric. It's a West End theater, although it's in Hammersmith.... *Tel 0181/741–2311; 0171/836–3464 (ticket agency). King St. W6, Hammersmith tube stop.*

Lyric Studio. The diffusion line of the above.... *Tel 0181/ 741–8701.*

Man in the Moon. Another pub fringe theater, this one in Chelsea.... *Tel 0171/351–2876. 392 Kings Rd. SW3, Sloane Square tube stop, then 11 or 22 bus.*

Midland Bank Student Theatreline. Call after 2pm for details of today's cut-rate student standby tickets.... *Tel 0171/379–8900.*

Minema. Sounds like a mini movie house? That's what it is, with big armchairs.... *Tel 0171/235–4225. Knightsbridge SW1, Knightsbridge tube stop.*

Movingstage Marionette Company. The stage moves because it's in a barge on the Regents Canal.... *Tel 0171/ 249–6876. Puppet Theatre Barge, Little Venice, Bloomfield Rd. W9, Warwick Road tube stop.*

NFT. What everyone calls the estimable, two-auditorium, National Film Theatre in the South Bank Centre. Every movie you ever loved, missed, or wondered what happened to turns up here sooner or later. Membership costs 40p/day.... *Tel 0171/928–3232. South Bank SE1, Waterloo tube stop.*

National Theatre. The South Bank Centre's trio of theaters (Olivier, Lyttelton, Cottesloe) are the playgrounds for the occasionally star-flecked, ever-changing, nearly always brilliant Royal National Theatre Company.... *Tel 0171/928– 2252. South Bank SE1, Waterloo tube stop.*

Notting Hill Carnival. The main event of London's grooviest neighborhood erupts around Ladbroke Grove during August Bank Holiday weekend—like Trinidad in the rain.

Odeon Marble Arch. The biggest screen—and movie theater— in town shows strictly Hollywood crowd-pleasers.... *Tel 0171/723–2011. Edgware Rd. W1, Marble Arch tube stop.*

Old Bull Arts Centre. If you can face the trek, this lively arty place is truly irreverent—lots of physical theater, "new circus," scurrilous musicals.... *Tel 0181/449–0048. 68 High St. Barnet EN5, High Barnet tube stop.*

Old Red Lion. Here's yet another pub theater in Islington, this one conveniently close to the tube stop.... *Tel 0171/837– 7816. St. John's St. N1, Angel tube stop.*

Old Vic. West End, but off the path, this stages consistent crowd-pleasers.... *Tel 0171/928–7616. Waterloo Rd. SE1, Waterloo tube stop.*

Orange Tree. It would help if you were somewhere near Richmond to get to this far-Off-West End theater.... *Tel 0181/ 940–3633. 1 Clarence St. Richmond, Richmond tube stop.*

Pippa Pop-ins. Possibly the world's only children's hotel, and certainly London's, will give the kids the night of their lives, and you a night of freedom.... *Tel 0171/385–2458. 430 Fulham Rd. SW6, Parsons Green tube stop.*

The Place. Is the place for contemporary dance—practically the center of the world for it.... *Tel 0171/387–0031. 17 Duke's Rd. WC1, Euston tube stop.*

Poetry Society. This is the nerve center of the establishment, somewhat impenetrable, but they can tell you about any festivals or special events.... *Tel 0171/240–4810. 22 Betterton St. WC2, Covent Garden tube stop.*

Polka Children's Theatre. A theater built just for kids, with play facilities and a toy shop, but not by night.... *Tel 0181/543–0363. 240 The Broadway SW19, Wimbledon South tube stop.*

Prince Charles. The bargain basement of West End movie theaters, where for a couple of quid you can catch those off-Hollywood movies you hated to miss.... *Tel 0171/437–8181. Leicester Place (off Leicester Square) WC2, Leicester Square tube stop.*

Pull My Daisy. Twice-a-week poetry slam, Tuesdays at Madame JoJo's (see The Club Scene), Thursdays at Mas Café.... *Tel 0171/243–0969. Mas Café, All Saints Rd. W11, Royal Oak tube stop.*

Purcell Room. See **South Bank Centre.**

Queen Elizabeth Hall. See **South Bank Centre.**

Regent's Park Open Air Theatre. London's version of Shakespeare in the Park takes place here. Quality productions; sometimes rain stops the play.... *Tel 0171/486–2431. Regent's Park NW1, Baker Street tube stop.*

Richmond Festival. This patrician neighborhood way upstream celebrates the arts for a week, with many events, usually in July.... *Tel 0181/332–0534.*

Rio Cinema. The East End representative of London's repertory cinema scene, in the neighborhood of the Hackney

Empire.... *Tel 0171/254–6677. Kindsland High St. E8, Dalston BR.*

Ritzy. And the South London version.... This Brixton landmark also shows first-run movies, but it's not worth coming all this way for those, unless you're going on to the Fridge or the Academy or the Mambo Inn.... *Tel 0171/737–2121. Brixton Oval, Coldharbour Lane SW2, Brixton tube stop.*

Riverside Studios. Theater and dance are happily showcased in this 20-odd-year-old Hammersmith arts center, with bar, cafe, and an excellent repertory cinema and art gallery on site. It's out of the way—a good 15-minute walk from the tube stop.... *Tel 0181/741–2255. Crisp Rd. W6, Hammersmith tube stop.*

Royal Academy of Music. Students and visiting alumni, plus other pros, often perform in its Dukes Hall.... *Tel 0171/935–5461. Marylebone Rd. NW1, Baker Street tube stop.*

Royal College of Music. The other school, with many excellent performances by maestri and divas of the future in its Britten Theatre.... *Tel 0171/589–3643. Prince Consort Rd. SW7, South Kensington tube stop.*

Royal Court. This West End theater made its name on ground-breaking programming (e.g., Osborne's *Look Back in Anger*).... *Tel 0171/730–1745. Sloane Square SW1, Sloane Square tube stop.*

Royal Court Theatre Upstairs. The still-groundbreaking studio version of the above stages all new plays.... *Tel 0171/730–2554.*

Royal Festival Hall. See **South Bank Centre.**

Royal Opera House. Where the Royal Opera Company and Royal Ballet both live. Expensive, world-class.... *Tel 0171/304–4000. Bow St. WC2, Covent Garden tube stop.*

Rudolph Steiner Theatre. Has a varied program related intimately to the teaching of the great educator and founder of anthroposophy, including performances of eurythmy.... *Tel 0171/723–4400. 35 Park Rd. NW1, Baker Street tube stop.*

St. George's Hanover Square. A visit-worthy neoclassical church with occasional concerts.... *Tel 0171/629–0874. St. George's St. W1, Oxford Circus tube stop.*

St. Giles in the Barbican. A city church with a classical concert program.... *No telephone. Fore St. EC2, Barbican tube stop.*

St. James's Garlickhythe. Another city church notable for its concerts.... *Tel 0171/236–1719, Garlick Hill EC4, Mansion House tube stop.*

St. John's Smith Square. BBC Radio often broadcasts concerts from this deconsecrated church, the major minor concert hall.... *Tel 0171/222–1061. Smith Square SW1, Westminster tube stop.*

St. Margaret's Westminster. In the shadow of Westminster Abbey is this lesser church, with its concert program.... *Tel 0171/222–5152. St. Margaret St. SW1, Westminster tube stop.*

St. Martin-in-the-Fields. Beautiful church, beautiful music. See if you can catch the Academy of St. Martin-in-the-Fields on its home turf.... *Tel 0171/839–8362. Trafalgar Square WC2, Charing Cross tube stop.*

St. Martins. Not a church—a theater, presenting *The Mousetrap* in its forty-millionth year.... *Tel 0171/836–1443. West St. WC2, Leicester Square tube stop.*

St. Peter's Eaton Square. Church concerts among some of London's priciest and most enviable real estate.... *Tel 0171/823–1205. Eaton Square SW1, Victoria tube stop.*

Sadler's Wells. This Islington theater is best known for dance but also transfers European theater and music productions.... *Tel 0171/278–8916. Rosebery Ave. EC1, Angel tube stop.*

Savoy. Built by Richard D'Oyly Carte of Gilbert and Sullivan fame, and adjacent to its namesake hotel, this West End theater was recently restored in deco style.... *Tel 0171/ 836–8888. Strand WC2, Charing Cross tube stop.*

Screen on Baker Street. One of a trio of comfortable, independent art-house theaters that have a hip young staff, and serve good cake.... *Tel 0171/935–2772. 96 Baker St. NW1, Baker Street tube stop.*

Screen on the Green. The original of the above-mentioned trio has loads of restaurants and bars in the neighborhood.... *Tel 0171/226–3520. Islington Green N1, Angel tube stop.*

Screen on the Hill. This Hill is five minutes downhill from Hampstead; the second in the chain of three.... *Tel 0171/435–3366. Haverstock Hill NW3, Belsize Park tube stop.*

Shaftsbury. A large and acoustically brilliant West End theater.... *Tel 0171/379–5399. 210 Shaftsbury Ave. WC2, Tottenham Court Road tube stop.*

Smiley's Cut Price Comedy Club. These cheap and funny Monday shows at the Hackney Emp look like they may become a permanent fixture. Call ahead just to make sure our prediction is right.... *Tel 0181/985–2424. 291 Mare SW8. Hackney Central BR.*

Society of London Theatre. SOLT is the body that collates information from all the West End houses, operates the Half Price Ticket Booth, and publishes the fortnightly *London Theatre Guide* (which you can subscribe to for around £23/year) and *The Complete Guide to London's West End Theatres*.... *Tel 0171/836–0971. Bedford Chambers, The Piazza, Covent Garden WC2E 8HQ.*

South Bank Centre. The center of mainstream-but-still-good—often *really* good—theater (see **National Theatre**, above), and classical music, at the three concert halls. Also catch the various free foyer exhibitions and happenings.... *Tel 0171/928–8800. South Bank SE1, Waterloo tube stop.*

Southwark Cathedral. London's oldest church after Westminster Abbey has a concert program.... *Tel 0171/407–2939. Winchester Walk, London Bridge tube stop.*

Stage Pass. Young people's (14—29) arts discount card. Well worth getting for the longer, culturally oriented sojourn.... *Tel 0171/379–6722. 28 Charing Cross Rd. WC2H 0DB.*

LONDON / THE ARTS

Theatre Royal Drury Lane. London's oldest and most haunted West End theater has been rebuilt three times; this fourth incarnation dates from 1812.... *Tel 0171/494–5000. Catherine St. WC2, Covent Garden tube stop.*

Theatre Royal Haymarket. Another old one, this has been a theater since 1720, with the present auditorium designed by John Nash in 1821.... *Tel 0171/930–8800. Haymarket SW1, Piccadilly Circus tube stop.*

Theatre Royal Stratford East. This Off–West End theater is hit-or-miss, since it stages a lot of brand-new work and young playwrights' stuff. When it hits, it's great.... *Tel 0181/534–0310. Gerry Raffles Square, E15, Stratford tube stop.*

Tom Allen Arts Centre. An East End fringe theater with a wide-ranging program of multi-ethnic, gender-bending, musical, dancey, dramatic events.... *Tel 0181/519–6818. Grove Crescent Rd. Stratford E15, Stratford BR.*

Tricycle. This well-loved Off–West End theater was almost closed due to lack of funds, but now thrives again.... *Tel 0171/328–1000. 269 Kilburn High Rd. NW6, Kilburn tube stop.*

UCI Whiteleys. The multi- to end all plexes, perched atop London's only true mall, with late-night shopping, and eight blockbuster screens.... *Tel 0171/792–3303. Queensway W2, Bayswater tube stop.*

Unicorn Theatre. The oldest children's theater in town, but sans evening performances, sadly.... *Tel 0171/836–3334. 6 Great Newport St. WC2, Leicester Square tube stop.*

Union Chapel. In Islington, a deconsecrated congregational church makes an acoustically and atmospherically lovely mostly jazz venue.... *Tel 0171/226–1686. Compton Terrace N1, Highbury and Islington tube stop.*

The Vortex. A cabaret-style cafe/bar home for modern jazz in far, funky Stokey—many veggie and ethnic restaurants nearby.... *Tel 0171/254–6516. Stoke Newington Church St. N16, Stoke Newington BR.*

Warner West End. London's largest movie multiplex. Nine screens, but you've either seen these flicks already, or have avoided them.... *Tel 0171/437–4347. Leicester Square WC2, Leicester Square tube stop.*

Watermans Arts Centre. This is a trek, but, like the Old Bull, worth it for anyone dedicated to innovative theater.... *Tel 0181/568–1176. 40 High St. Brentford, Kew Bridge BR.*

Waterstone's. One of the country's biggest book chains has author signings and evening readings in many branches, including this one.... *Tel 0171/434–4291. 121—129 Charing Cross Rd. WC2, Tottenham Court Road tube stop.*

Wembley Stadium/Wembley Arena. The big ones play here.... *Tel 0181/900–1234. Empire Way, Wembley Middlesex, Wembley Park tube stop.*

Westminster Abbey. The exquisite center of London, founded by Edward the Confessor in 1040 (or King Sebert in the 7th century, no one's sure) houses heavenly concerts, sometimes featuring its choristers. Henry Purcell played its organ.... *Tel 0171/222–7110. 20 Dean's Yard SW1, Westminster tube stop.*

Wigmore Hall. This lovely, recently restored concert hall behind Oxford Street has a really accessible program.... *Tel 0171/935–2141. 36 Wigmore St. W1, Bond Street tube stop.*

Young Vic. An excellent Off–West End theater with two auditoriums.... *Tel 0171/928–6363. 66 The Cut SE1, Waterloo tube stop.*

LONDON ⌣ THE ARTS

spo

rts

4

Most Londoners like
watching other people do
sports more than they like
doing them themselves.
The sports they like best to
watch are those two most
British of games, football

(soccer, not gridiron) and cricket, which are as different as their playing seasons (winter; summer). So are their styles of spectatorship. The traditional football fan is a beer-swilling, scarf-waving yobbo, while the cricket enthusiast is a plummy tea-sipping gent in a flannel blazer. We don't say much about cricket here, because cricket is a day game. So are rugby and racing, which bring up the rear as the Londoner's favorite sports, though anything may have happened by now to Rugby Union, which went professional at the beginning of 1996, thus losing its purity. Horse racing happens out of town, but there's an inner-London alternative in greyhound racing, and a night at the dogs is splendid entertainment, at which you get to drink beer and gamble simultaneously. In fact, beer and sport go together like chalk and pool tables in a country which routinely produces champion darts and snooker players. Basketball and ice hockey (hockey here denotes *field* hockey) are not so expertly played, but they are improving, along with their sponsorship.

The Lowdown

Where to watch

Basketball... The **Budweiser League** is the best of British basketball, boosted by a late-eighties boom. Still, don't expect NBA action, not even from local stars **Crystal Palace**, nor the winningest team, **London Towers**, although the show-bizzy East End Leopards, complete with their Wildcats cheerleaders and clubby soundtrack, make a good night out. Emotions run highest in October for the McDonalds Championship battle fought at the **London Arena** (tel 0171/515–8515, Limeharbour E14; Crossharbour DLR) and from January for the Budweiser Championship fixtures at **Wembley Exhibition Centre** (tel 0181/900–1234, Empire Way; Wembley Park tube). Speaking of the NBA, London (well, Stockport, actually) exported starter **John Amaechi** to the Cleveland Cavaliers, while the '89 Lakers sent England player **Steve Bucknall** back to London Towers after 29 games. Look out for star Leopards "Downtown" Karl Brown and Ian "Dynamite" White (he's 7'1").

Cricket... The national sport of summer, with its picturesque whites and euphonious *thwack* of leather on willow, is a daytime game.

Darts... It's a stretch to consider darts a sport, but this game is taken very seriously in the land of the pub. The **Embassy World Professional Championship** is the British Darts Organisation's zenith, while the glitzier renegade **World Darts Council**'s Skol-sponsored **World Championship** is staged later, and boasts the superstar "athletes" of the sport, Jocky Wilson, Eric Bristow, John Lowe, and Phil Taylor. Although these winter tournaments are held outside London, they're worth catching on TV for the comedy value of extremely fat men throwing feathered pins at a circle while a sellout crowd holds its breath.

Football... Football, which is what you'll have to call soccer while in London, is usually played in the afternoon, but if there happens to be a night game during your visit (every newspaper lists the games), go. It's an electrifying spectacle. Do wear the right colors, since London fans are insanely partisan, and occasionally violent, with **Millwall** followers having the worst rep for Actual Bodily Harm. Their new stadium, **The Den** (tel 0171/231–9999, Senegal Fields, Zanpa Rd. SE16; South Bermondsey BR from Waterloo), has calmed them down, perhaps because it has more toilets than any other major stadium. Millwall plays, along with fellow South Londoners **Crystal Palace** (tel 0181/771–8841, Selhurst Park, Park Rd. SE25; Selhurst BR from Victoria), in what used to be called the Second Division, but is now the **Endsleigh Insurance League First Division**. The rest of the London teams play elite footie in the liquor-sponsored **FA Carling Premiership**. They are: **Tottenham Hotspur**, or the Spurs (tel 0181/365–5050, White Hart Lane, 748 High Rd. N17; White Hart Lane BR from Liverpool Street), the Gunners, **Arsenal** (tel 0171/354–5404, Avenell Rd. N5; Arsenal tube stop), the Blues, **Chelsea** (tel 0171/385–5545, Stamford Bridge, Fulham Rd. SW6; Fulham Broadway tube stop), **QPR**, Queens Park Rangers (tel 0181/740–0610, Rangers Stadium, South Africa Rd. W12; White City tube stop), and the Hammers, **West Ham United** (tel 0181/548–2700; Boleyn Ground, Green St. E13; Upton Park tube). You'd be lucky to have a choice of games, but if you do, Chelsea, Arsenal, and QPRs' grounds are the most central.

Greyhound racing... Watching a pack of skinny dogs run round in circles chasing the smell of rabbit is enormous fun, and London's clutch of greyhound stadia provides a classic sporting night out. The best is the expensively rebuilt **London Stadium Hackney** (tel 0181/986–3511, Waterden Rd. E15; Hackney Wick BR, North London Line), where you can have a decent meal and a bottle of wine in the upstairs restaurant, watching close-ups of the track action on your table TV, while your personal Tote Runner places your bets. You can also swill beer and lurch around downstairs for a more authentic experience. Other dog tracks are the well-known **Wembley** (tel 0181/902–8833; Wembley Park tube stop), **Walthamstow** (tel 0181/531–4255; Chigford Rd. E4; Highams Park BR from Liverpool Street), **Catford** (tel 0181/690–2261, Adenmore Rd. SE6; Catford Bridge BR from Charing Cross), and **Wimbledon** (tel 0181/946–5361, Plough Lane SW19; Wimbledon Park tube stop). They're all horribly hard to get to, so invest your winnings in a cab.

Ice hockey... The **British League** has progressed hugely in the few years of its existence, from nothing at all to a bit. However, you'd still have to be a potential sponsor to trek to places like the out-of-town **Ice Bowl** (tel 01634/388477, Ambley Rd, Gillingham Business Park, Surrey; Gillingham BR from Charing Cross). If you're accustomed to NHL razzmatazz and quality, the amateurish atmosphere is quaint—or depressing.

Rugby... It's hard to say where rugby will be by the time you read this, since the amateur game, the 15-a-side **Rugby Union**, is going professional before our very eyes. London stars the **Saracens**, into which £2.5 million (big bucks for British sport) was poured, are getting promoted like a new movie, while their Twickenham brethren the **Harlequins** are planning a new 20,000-seat stadium. Top teams play in the **Courage National League** and the newish **European Super League**. The game resembles American football without padding, played by men with quadriceps the size of waists, who sing ditties with filthy lyrics ("rugby songs") in the showers. It's an upper-class sport played at public (=exclusive, private) school, and it's also the passion of the entire Welsh nation. Since night games are rare, we note only that the Saracens' home is the **Bramley Ground** (tel 0181/449–3770, Chase Side N14; Cockfosters tube stop).

Tennis... What everybody wants in the last week of June and first week of July is **Wimbledon** tickets. Well, sorry, but those are allocated on a lottery system in January (to join in, write, and include a self-addressed stamped envelope, from October through December: All England Lawn Tennis & Croquet Club, Box 98, Church Rd., Wimbledon SW19 5AE). However, you can easily get to see even the hallowed **Centre Court** by lining up for admission to the grounds,

LONDON ⟨ SPORTS

then going for the standing room, or—more pertinent for nighttime viewing—buying the secondhand tickets of people who left early, which are collected and sold (inexpensively) for charity. Note that during the first week, it's a cinch to see Grand Slam, big-shot players up real close on the outer courts (01839/123417, info line, during the fortnight, 49p/min charged, or 0181/946–2244; Church Rd., Wimbledon SW19; Southfields tube stop).

Where to play

Aerobics... See "Gyms," below.

Bowling... This is beginning to catch on in London, and the biggest provider of lanes (24 of them) is usually thronged with keglers. **Rowans Tenpin Bowl** (tel 0181/800–1950, Stroud Green Rd. N4; Finsbury Road tube stop) has the advantage of being open practically all night Saturday, and till 3am the rest of the week, and the disadvantage of being in a hideous part of North London. The other place to score a strike or two is more accessibly at Queen's Ice Skating Club (see "Ice Skating," below).

Boxing... One of the most fun and unusual ways to spend a sweaty evening in London is to submit to the grueling two-hour, no-contact **KO Circuit** at **All Stars Gym** (tel 0181/960–7724, 576 Harrow Rd. W10; call after 5pm; Monday through Friday 7:30pm–9:30; Westbourne Park tube stop), **Isola Akay**'s wonderful West London amateur gym housed in a deconsecrated church. All contenders, male, female (the ratio is about 4:1), beginner, and fighter are welcome, and invited to tea and biscuits afterwards. Or do some Jeet Kune Do in friendly, bald martial arts master Bob Breen's converted school building, **The Academy** (tel 0171/729–5789, 16 Hoxton Square N1; Old Street tube stop).

Dance... You need to buy a day membership for the excellent classes at both **Pineapple** (tel 0171/836–4004, 7 Langley St. WC2; Covent Garden tube stop) and **Danceworks** (tel 0171/629–6183, 16 Balderton St. W1; Bond Street tube stop). Pineapple tends toward the aerobics, hip-hop, jazz side, while Danceworks has classes in everything from ballet to line dancing at all grades from beginner to pro, plus various aerobics innovations, like "Kickaerobics," and has more later classes. If you are a pro, and need to take class, try **The Place** (tel 0171/388–8430, 17 Dukes Rd. WC2; Euston tube stop), which is attached to the London Contemporary Dance School, and its theater.

Gyms... Gyms in the center of town, with temporary memberships, include the trusty **Central YMCA** (tel 0171/637–8131, 112 Great Russell St. WC1; Tottenham Court Road tube stop), which, like every Y, is very well equipped, though frill-free. Better looking are the three City of Westminster Council-owned multifacility sports centers, which boast branded up-to-the-minute gyms called **Courtney's** (or "Life Fitness Personal Performance Centres," to give their full title). These have all the weights and cardio things you could wish for, they're bargains at around a fiver a day, they're open until about 9pm, and there's a program of classes (extra charge), too. The best classes are in the **Move It** program at the **Seymour Leisure Centre** (tel 0171/402–5795, Seymour Place W2; Marylebone tube stop). The other central Courtneys with aerobics are the **Marshall Street Leisure Centre** (tel 0171/287–1022, 14–16 Marshall St., Soho W1; Oxford Circus tube stop) and the **Porchester Centre** (tel 0171/792–2919, Queensway W2; Bayswater tube stop). Also a bargain, and also easily found—slap in the middle of Covent Garden— is **Jubilee Hall** (tel 0171/379–0008, 30 The Piazza, WC2; Covent Garden tube stop), where you can do *wu shu* (Chinese boxing) before your step class. Nearby is the more expensive but elysian **Gym at the Sanctuary** (tel 0171/240–0695, 11 Floral St. WC2; Covent Garden tube stop), attached to the women-only day spa of the same name, but operated separately—a good one for women to sweat unobserved by Schwarzeneggers. For said Schwarzeneggers, the **Albany Fitness Centre** (tel 0171/383–7131, St. Bede's Church, Albany St. NW1; Great Portland Street tube stop) is fun and full of hardware. It's a deconsecrated church, and offers day memberships, which surprisingly few serious weight-training gyms do.

Pool... The pub is many a Londoner's social center, and many a pub has at least one pool table. Stumble upon the right night, and you'll be amazed at the Fast Eddie Felson standard of play and the serious competitiveness, which embrace both interpub league battles and unofficial—

LONDON SPORTS

well, illegal, actually—gambling (I once saw a £1000 bet on a single frame). To join in, write your name at the end of the list on the blackboard, or place your coins at the end of the queue at the side of the table. When your turn comes up—and that takes all night on weekends at a popular pool pub—you play the previous winner. Lose, and join the back of the queue again; beat them, and you "stay on" until you're beaten. Hustlers be warned, British rules are *completely* different from those in America. In fact, the whole game is different. The cue ball ("the white") is smaller; solids are called "spots"; you don't call your shot (except on the 8-ball—"the black"—in some pubs); scratch, and you give your opponent an extra shot. In fact, you'd better watch and ask, and read the rules on the wall. If you'd rather play amongst yourselves, go very early, or skip the pub and hit a club. **Rowans Tenpin Bowl** (tel 0181/800–1950, Stroud Green Rd. N4; Finsbury Road tube stop) has 24-hour pool tables, and no membership fee. More central by far is the **Centre Point Snooker Club** (tel 0171/240–6886, Centre Point, New Oxford St. WC1; Tottenham Court Road tube stop), where you pay £2 for a day membership, and can play till 6am; while over in trendyland, the **Camden Snooker Centre** (tel 0171/485–6094, 16 Delancey St. NW1; Camden Town tube stop) demands you buy an annual membership at 12 quid, but you get to play in the dark alongside stars of Britpop until 6:30am. Those last two specialize in the grown-up and far more difficult version of pool—snooker. At the cyborg-styled **Elbow Room** (tel 0171/221–5211, 103 Westbourne Grove W2; Westbourne Park tube stop), however, pool (on gray baize) is king, and burgers, sausage sandwiches, and "Cajun chicken livers with curry coconut sauce" are served with beer and cocktails until 11:30pm nightly.

Rock climbing... That isn't a misprint. There are three places to do this at night. The star is the **NLRC** (tel 0181/980–0289, Cordova Rd. Bow E3; Mile End tube stop), which stands, thrillingly, if misleadingly, for "North London Rescue Commando." It's hidden deep in the East End (call for directions), but worth the trek for rock fans, since there are indoor faces of many features—for bouldering (traverse climbing), competition climbing (with movable holds), and high-up, medium, easy, impossible, and completely upside-down climbing. There are lessons, and it's all extremely inexpensive. The newest wall is outdoors at the **Westway Sports Centre** (tel 0181/969–0992, 1 Crowthorne Rd. W10; Latimer Road tube stop), with a 15-meter tower, a 12-meter pyramid, and 30 meters of traversing wall. This, too, is cheap to use (both cost well under £5 a day), and there are lessons. One more indoor wall is found in North London at the **Sobell Centre** (tel 0171/609–2166, Hornsey Rd. N7; Finsbury Park tube stop). It's a good 70 feet tall, and can be combined with the many other sports here, including squash and ice-skating.

Running... The great London parks, which are underused by runners, are officially closed after dark. At high summer, that gives you till around 10pm to do the 3.5-mile **Hyde Park** loop, entering at Speaker's Corner (Marble Arch tube), following Park Lane south to Hyde Park Corner, then running the banks of the Serpentine and Long Water lakes, and returning the same way; or the 4.5-mile perimeter of Hyde Park and Kensington Gardens, starting at the Bayswater Road Black Lion Gate (Queensway tube) and the Broad Walk. You can also do the 2.5-mile **Regent's Park Outer Circle** loop (Regent's Park) anytime, and back in the West End, there's a gorgeous 2.5-miler around the edges of **Green Park** and **St. James's Park**, whose scenery includes Buckingham Palace, which never closes. If you don't like to run alone, join the **Bow Street Runners'** weekly evening run from **Jubilee Hall** (30 Covent Garden Piazza WC2, Covent Garden tube stop; call Jane for details at 0171/939–8577. If you do like to run alone, London provides safe and varied terrain. Try the Upper, Lower, and Chiswick **Malls** (nothing to do with shopping, they rhyme with "pals") from **Hammersmith Bridge** (Hammersmith tube stop) for an unusual mile, or an intermittently crowded, insanely scenic 1.5 miles on the **Victoria Embankment** from Westminster (Westminster tube stop), across Waterloo Bridge, past the South Bank Centre on Riverside Walk, and back across Westminster Bridge to the Houses of Parliament. Best of all, just jog the streets wherever you are, clocking your own distance by time. This is most fun in **residential neighborhoods** at twilight, before the drapes are drawn, when cozily lit domestic scenes flash past like snapshots.

Skating... Since Britain has produced a few ice-dance champs, you'd expect the capital's rinks to be spectacular. They're not. Still, a night at the biggest central rink, **Queens Ice Skating Club** (tel 0171/229–0172, Queensway W2; Queensway tube stop) is O.K., with its disco, classes, and skates for rent. There is, however, no hockey, and hockey skates are never allowed on regular rinks. At the fall- and winter-only **Broadgate Arena** (tel 0171/588–6565, 3 Broadgate EC2; Liverpool Street tube stop) in a swanky City business development, you can substitute stupid games like brushball (it is what it sounds like), some of which aren't even played in skates. Otherwise, just go round and round and round on London's only outdoor rink, which stays open late Fridays. It's small—as is the indoor rink at the **Sobell Centre** (tel 0171/609–2166, Hornsey Rd. N7; Finsbury Park tube stop). Travel out a bit further, and up to one of London's highest points at **Alexandra Palace** (tel 0181/365–2121, Alexandra Park N22; Wood Green tube stop), for London's biggest rink, and one of its best views.

Squash... Squash is what you'll find here instead of racquetball, and clubs where you can play (though not reserve by phone) without joining include **Ironmonger Row** (tel 0171/253–4011, Ironmonger Row EC1; Old Street tube stop), **Portobello Green** (tel 0181/960–2221, 3–5 Thorpe Close W10; Latimer Road tube stop) and the **Sobell Sports Centre** (tel 0171/609–2166, Hornsey Rd. N7; Finsbury Park tube stop). You can also play **badminton** there, and at the **Seymour Leisure Centre** (tel 0171/402–5795, Seymour Place W2; Marylebone tube stop).

Swimming... Most of London's many public swimming pools stay open at least some evenings. On the whole, they're well-maintained and sparkly clean, though the chlorine level is high, and the changing rooms are communal. Most of the best lap pools are slightly outside the center of town, but the **Seymour Leisure Centre** (tel 0171/402–5795, Seymour Place W2; Marylebone tube stop) has a good, long four-laner, and is a 15-minute walk from Marble Arch. Watch out for aquaerobics times, though. Ditto the **Marshall Street Leisure Centre** (tel 0171/287–1022, 14 Marshall St. W1; Oxford Circus tube stop). The **Oasis** (tel 0171/831–1804, 32 Endell St. WC2; Tottenham Court Road tube stop) has two pools—

one outdoors—and couldn't be more central, but every office worker near Covent Garden is decanted inside during lunchtimes. **Swiss Cottage** pool (tel 0171/586–5989, Winchester Rd. NW3; Swiss Cottage tube stop) is one of the biggest (37 yards long), and conveniently next to the tube stop, but it also gets crowded. Almost as big are pools at **Ironmonger Row** (tel 0171/253–4011, Ironmonger Row EC1; Old Street tube stop) and at the **Porchester Centre** (tel 0171/792–2919, Queensway W2; Bayswater tube stop), which has adults-only and women-only evening swim sessions. Really late-night swimmers will have had the forethought to book into a hotel with a pool bigger than the jacuzzi. The best are at **Grosvenor House** (tel 0171/499–6363, Park Lane W1; Marble Arch tube stop) and **Kensington Close** (tel 0171/937–8170, Wrights Lane W8; High Street Kensington tube stop), with **Champney's at Le Meridien** (tel 0171/734–8000, Piccadilly W1; Piccadilly Circus tube stop) having the poshest, complete with palm fronds, and not small at 12 square meters; the **Berkeley** (tel 0171/235–6000, Wilton Place SW3; Knightsbridge tube stop) has the most gorgeous summer pool, with a removable roof.

Tennis... Year-round evening play is possible at the **Islington Tennis Centre** (tel 0171/700–1370, Market Rd. N7; Caledonian Road tube stop), and at the **Westway Sports Complex** (tel 0181/969–0992, 1 Crowthorne Rd. W10; Latimer Road tube stop). Both also have outdoor courts, but there are more picturesque examples of these to be found in various parks, especially **Holland Park** (tel 0171/602–2226, Holland Park tube stop) and **Regents Park** (tel 0171/724–0643, Camden Town tube stop). They're seasonal, though. Fees for play at all these sites tend to be around £5 per hour.

Yoga... London's best and finest-looking yoga school is the Notting Hill Gate **Life Centre** (tel 0171/221–4602, 15 Edge St. W8; Notting Hill Gate tube stop), where very bendy Godfrey Devereux and staff teach various levels of the energetic Vinyasa technique, and the latest class starts at 8pm Monday through Thursday. The **Seymour Leisure Centre** (tel 0171/402–5795, Seymour Place W2; Marylebone tube stop) and **Jubilee Hall** (tel 0171/379–0008, 30 The Piazza WC2; Covent Garden tube stop) have more general evening yoga classes.

hangi

ng out

5

London's a fairly challenging place for the visitor who's looking to do nothing. It's a problem that arises from the climate, and it's compounded by the sitting-room culture that makes London a terrific place to hang out in for the locals, but which limits slacking options for the out-of-towner. Hanging out happens behind closed doors, around the kitchen table or fireplace, at dinner parties, over late-night tea. Luckily, continental street life has made inroads into the traditional British indoor soul, the come-in-out-of-the-rain, batten-down-the-hatches-and-put-on-the-slippers mentality that has so often made London so dull.

Walking, a prime low-concept pastime, has always been good in London, so long as you're not fussed about a little drizzle. Distances are long, and the geography is convoluted, mind you, so remember the *A to Z*, and don't be too ambitious about covering the miles. What's best about a London walk, especially one after dark in a quiet neighborhood, is the sudden surprising detail—an alley or mews, a spotlit church gargoyle, somebody's sitting room with curtains undrawn, a secret garden. Parts of the city are practically rural—Hampstead is the quintessential London village—while others are edgy and urban, like King's Cross. From King's Cross to Hampstead is a couple of hours' walk, and this is why you should consider strolling a legitimate way to spend time. Here are some suggestions for those evening strolls, along with other nighttime activities that don't fit into the other usual categories, from view-finding and bus-hopping to shopping, window shopping…and gambling.

The Lowdown

Walkies... If you just want a minor stroll in town, connect up the grand West End squares—**Grosvenor**, where the U.S. Embassy stands, and **Berkeley**, where the nightingale sang—then take Curzon Street down to the picturesque tangle of alleys, **Shepherd's Market**—the site of the May Fair which gave this neighborhood its name. You emerge on Piccadilly, across the street from **Green Park**. Or start at the big daddy of piazzas, **Trafalgar Square**, and head toward the Thames down Whitehall, with the **Houses of Parliament** at the end—impressive at night when floodlit, with "Big Ben's" famous, green-tinged (thanks to its new energy-efficient lighting) clock faces. Pass—admiringly—floodlit **Westminster Abbey** to visit Rodin's *Burghers of Calais* at **Victoria Tower Gardens**, then come back to **Westminster Bridge** to walk along Victoria Embankment to **Embankment Gardens**. Extend the walk by crossing the Hungerford Bridge (for trains and people only) to **Jubilee Gardens** for a peerless view back across to the north bank, and a further walk downstream, past the **South Bank Centre**, and, if you like, as far as **Tower Bridge**. Upstream, there's a perfect summertime stroll along **Hammersmith Mall**, stopping at the several pubs with outside tables. Another walk that is extra-atmospheric after dark is in and around **Lincoln's Inn Fields**, which is surrounded by the beautiful 17th-century courts of law (go the first Tuesday of the month, and get into Sir John Soane's Museum, too; see "Late Museums," below). Duck into any parts of the four **Inns of Court** (Gray's Inn, Lincoln's Inn, Middle and Inner Temples) you find open, just following your nose—it's a fascinating district. Nearby, **Bloomsbury** makes a handy adjunct to a theater visit or Covent Garden meal, with the **University of London** buildings, the **British Museum**, and many **Blue Plaques** to spot, particularly those of the Bloomsbury Group—Virginia Woolf, the Bells and Dora Carrington, T. S. Eliot and E. M. Forster, John Maynard Keynes, Lytton Strachey, et al.—who lived, wrote, and regarded themselves highly in…Bloomsbury. There are about 400 of these cerulean ceramic disks in London, stuck on house fronts of dead celebs who "enhanced human welfare or happiness." A few more walks out of the thousand possibilities: Start at **Notting Hill Gate**, window shop for antiques down Kensington Church Street to Kensington High Street, then follow tiny Derry Street for a turn around stunning 18th-century **Kensington Square**. Or do St. James's: from Green Park tube, take Queen's Walk (to the right of the Ritz) into the park, until you reach the tiny secret tunnel on the left, which will bring you in a winding fashion onto St. James's Street. Now explore east on Pall Mall with its elegant Edwardian clubs, via King Street to leafy **St. James's Square**—laid out around 1670—and down Jermyn Street, for window shopping of a gentlemanly bent.

Walkies on a leash… If you're the sort who likes to know exactly where you are, try an **Original London Walks** (tel 0171/624–3978; P.O. Box 1708, NW6) walk. Taverns on their pub crawls are "like precious gems in rumpled velvet," they say, with tongue just far enough in cheek to be witty but not cynical. Their walks are as much about the incidental history and context as the destinations, and you get to see historic parts in detail. And their "Jack the Ripper Haunts" walk is the best of many copycats. When dusk is late, another variety of packaged walk is available at **Kew Gardens** (tel 0181/940–1171; Kew, Richmond, Surrey; Kew Gardens tube. Daily 9:30–dusk), where the 40,000 kinds of plants in 300 acres and the Victorian crystal palace greenhouses look beautiful in the sunset. A pair of free leaflets worth scoring are the Society of London Theatre's "**A Walk of Theatreland**" and "**The London Silver Jubilee Walkway**" map. Get them from London Tourist Board places; the first is also in leaflet spots around the West End—try theaters or the Mountbatten Hotel's lobby (tel 0171/340–3540; Seven Dials, Covent Garden WC2).

Night visions… Extend that first stroll (see Walkies, above) into Green Park, and walk across to **St. James's**

Park for a tree-framed view of all the famous buildings around there, floodlit over the lake—a heavenly scene. The aforementioned **Inns of Court** is also one of the most picturesque parts of the city, full of sudden vistas, labyrinthine passageways, great buildings, and green spaces. At the opposite extreme, the best wide-open spaces with glorious panoramas of the London skyline at night are **Parliament Hill Fields**, which is part of the Heath (Hampstead—whenever a Londoner refers to "the Heath," you may assume it's this), and **Primrose Hill** nearby. They're safe enough at night, though you should know that the former is London's premier summertime gay cruising ground.

Architectural moments... The tallest building here is Cesar Pelli's 50-storey tower at **1 Canada Square**, which is the centerpiece of London's weirdest square mile, **Canary Wharf** (tel 0171/418–2000 by day for info; Visitor Center, Cabot Place E. E14). Modeled on an American downtown, this business district reclaimed from slum ignominy as part of the 1980s redevelopment of Docklands never really fit in or took off here, but it makes a really offbeat evening outing, from deserted mall to riverside pub to a Cabot Hall concert. The building to see when down this way is Nicholas Grimshaw's multi-prize-winning **Financial Times Print Works** (240 East India Dock Rd. E14), which is spectacular at night, with the giant whirring presses visible through one vast plate of glass. Another voguish building best seen at night is Richard Rogers' 1986 inside-out glass and steel **Lloyd's Tower** (tel 0171/623–7100; 1 Lime St.; closed to visitors), which has the best electric-blue floodlighting. At the opposite extreme, the foundations of the **Temple of Mithras** have sat on Queen Victoria Street since they were dug up in 1954, and below it, since it was built by the worshipers of Christ's third- and fourth-century rival, Mithras, Persian god of light. This, plus Christopher Wren's **Monument** (tel 0171/626–2717; Monument St.), and his masterpiece, the floodlit **St. Paul's Cathedral**— instantly recognizable as one of the defining buildings of the London skyline—are the City buildings most worth gazing on by night, when the streets are bereft of people.

Neighborhoods for nights... There's activity all around **Butler's Wharf**, where the Design Museum and Tower

Bridge are attractions by day, but the **Gastrodrome**, with all its offshoots, is the evening star (see Shopping), and there are increasing numbers of salubrious, expensive housing enclaves to nose around before riverside cocktails at **Le Pont de la Tour** (tel 0171/403–9403; 36D Shad Thames SE1). **Notting Hill** has abundant restaurants and bars, more or less clustered around the daytime center of Portobello Market. The former ganja-dealing yardie haunt, now restaurant- and cafe-laden **All Saints Road** is one hub; another is **Kensington Park Road**, from Lancaster Road almost up to Notting Hill Gate, then there's The Cow corner of **Westbourne Grove**. It hosts London's best and biggest party, the Notting Hill Carnival—a true Caribbean carnival that goes on for three days. It once had a reputation for trouble, but the worst you'll have to deal with is the crush of huge crowds. Meanwhile, up north, an evening stroll in expensive, vil-lagey, leaf-laden **Hampstead** might lead to a show at the sweet, old-fashioned repertory cinema, the Everyman, or a drink in a pub garden (or 'round the open fire). Contrastingly, **Camden Town**, straight down Haverstock Hill from there, is crammed with kids aged 18 to 30, pubs, music venues, bars, stores (some open late on weekends, but most are daytime only), restaurants, and more kids. From Camden Lock, you can walk along the canal tow-path in either direction—west to **Little Venice**, a gracious but very boring place, or east to **King's Cross**, which is the seediest part of town—prostitution, drug dealing, the lot. The nasty stuff happens around the British Rail Station, but there's another scene emerging behind it in the ware-houses, at places like Bagley's and the Cross—a youthful, artsy, clubbing one. Back in safe and wealthy boroughs, **Chelsea** is good for strolling, among former studios of the original bohemian Chelsea artists, past Wren's Royal Hospital and along Cheyne Walk, but it's better after dark for a certain style of singles-y bar hopping (wear comfort-able shoes—it's not compact).

Best bus routes… Climb the stairs to the top deck, show your Travelcard, and sit back for the least expensive grandstand tour in the land. Good bus routes include the **12**, for Holland Park to Hyde Park on the north side, Oxford and Regent streets, Piccadilly Circus, Trafalgar Square, and across Westminster Bridge; the **22** for the

King's Road, Chelsea, through to Knightsbridge, Hyde Park Corner, and Piccadilly; the **77**, which goes the length of the Albert Embankment and Lambeth Palace Road, with fab views of Westminster, ending at the South Bank Centre, or the **77a**, which mirrors that route on the left bank, taking Millbank past the Tate Gallery to Westminster, then climbing Whitehall and traversing the Strand to the heart of theaterland at the Aldwych. The **42** crosses Tower Bridge, having started at Liverpool Street Station, while the **133** does a similar City route, but crossing London Bridge, the next bridge along, for a good view of Tower Bridge (sit on the left side). A bus map is well worth getting, especially since it costs nothing.

Buses for insomniacs... 'Round midnight, buses sprout an "N" prefix and change their routes. Your Travelcard is no use now unless it's longer than a one-day one, and you'll find fares have doubled. But if you've no other plans, or are sleepless in the small hours, an impromptu top-deck odyssey shows you parts of the city that other methods can't reach. The above routes have their night versions, namely the **N12**; the **N19** for the Chelsea-to-Piccadilly 22; the **N77** for the 77a; and the **N44** for the 77's south-bank view of Westminster. No night bus crosses Tower Bridge, but the **N89** nips across London Bridge, goes through the deserted nighttime City to High Holborn, then joins the **N12** on Oxford Street. Many night buses have routes that go the distance, exploring the furthest reaches of the four compass points, and the vast majority of them reach their zenith at Trafalgar Square, mecca of the N-route, where insomniacs and clubbers collide.

Late museums... The **Victoria and Albert Musuem**, known to all as the V&A (tel 0171/938–8500; Cromwell Rd. SW7), is the national shrine of the decorative arts, with everything from the Shakespeare-immortalized Great Bed of Ware to last year's Lacroix and Comme in the famous Dress Collection. It started its Late View Wednesdays only recently, with 6:30-to-9:30pm opening hours, live music, wine bars in the galleries that are open (a revolving selection), free gallery talks, plus, for extra money, a buffet supper in the restaurant and a lecture. The unmissable **National Gallery** (tel 0171/839–3321; Trafalgar Sq. WC2), which has the, yes, national collection of eight centuries of Western European painting, needn't be missed by night owls during summer, when it also opens Wednesdays (to 8pm). And the other big one to do evenings is the **British Museum** (tel 0171/636–1555; Great Russell St. WC1), which has centuries and miles of exquisite and breathtaking objets, starring sculptures from the Parthenon and a lot of mummies. Its evenings don't usually offer all-area access, however, but tend to be special exhibition events, with an admission charge. London's most fun small museum, **Sir John Soane's Museum** (tel 0171/430–0175; Lincoln's Inn Fields WC2), the phantasmagorical dream house of the Bank of England's architect, full of antiquities, paintings, drawings, arresting colors and perspectives, is open 6 to 9pm on the month's first Tuesday. Other than these, pickings are slim, but museum evenings are bound to catch on now that they've started.

Shops of the evening... The entire West End—that's Oxford Street and environs in this context—has its late night on Thursday, when the big department stores—including **Selfridges** (tel 0171/629–1234; 400 Oxford St. W1; open till 8pm), **John Lewis** (tel 0171/629–7711; 278–306 Oxford St. W1; open till 8pm), and **Liberty** (tel 0171/734–1234; Regent St. W1; open till 7:30pm)—and boutiques, like high-end fashion haven **Browns** (tel 0171/491–7833; 23–27 South Molton St. W1; open till 7pm), the mid-to-highish-priced French chain **Joseph** (tel 0171/629–3713; 23 Old Bond St. W1; open till 7pm), and quality of-the-moment own-label plus young Euro designers hot spot **Whistles** (tel 0171/487–4484; 12–14 St. Christopher's Place W1; open till 7pm), don't close until 7 or 8pm. The British chain store that has a religious and countrywide following for its underwear, woollies, and food halls especially (ask an expat Brit what they miss about the U.K.; "M&S knickers," they'll reply...), **Marks & Spencer** (tel 0171/487–4484; 458 Oxford St. W1; open till 7pm Mon–Wed, Sat; till 8pm Thur and Fri) has more generous late nights, and the branch in the **Whiteleys Shopping Centre** (tel 0171/792–3332; Queensway W2) stays open till 10pm. Over in Knightsbridge, the other fashion-heavy professional-shoppers' heaven, late night is Wednesday, when the five floors of clothes in store-of-stores, **Harvey Nichols** (tel 0171/235–

5000; 109–125 Knightsbridge SW1) stay accessible until 8pm (it's 7pm here other weekdays), and that infamous tourist attraction of a department store, **Harrods** (tel 0171/730–1234; 87 Brompton Rd. SW1) invites you to stay till 7pm—on Thursday and Friday, too. Shophounds who don't call 8pm late night will find London frustrating. You can get CDs till midnight at **Tower** (tel 0171/439–2500; 1 Piccadilly Circus W1), or books until 10pm at the **Bookshop Islington Green** (tel 0171/359–4699; 76 Upper St. N1) if you happen to be up north, but there is not much midnight merchandise here. You could always stay up all night Thursday and hit the best antiques market in town when the stall holders set up around 4am at **Bermondsey Market** (Bermondsey Sq. SE10).

Shut shops... The streets with the best shop windows are predictable, but here's the list: **Bond Street** is top, and you can follow it from Piccadilly all the way up to **Oxford Street**, at which point the windows go tawdry—apart from Selfridges—or hang a left down Brook Street, and a right into pedestrian-only **South Molton Street**, across Oxford Street and catercorner into Gees Court and **St. Christopher's Place**. That will access the most expensive boutiques and a lot of jewels. The other window-shopping neighborhood is **Knightsbridge**, where you could start at the tube, and Harvey Nicholls, which has some fabulous designers do its vitrines, and—ignoring Sloane Street, where the boutiques are the crème de la crème, but their windows are kinda dull—head towards Harrods, hanging a left down little **Beauchamp Place** and **Walton Street**.

Night talks... The Wren church **St. James's Piccadilly** (tel 0171/437–5053; 197 Piccadilly W1) was his last (1684) and his favorite, and has a fiberglass spire, thanks to the Blitz. Learn to read the tarot, attend guru seminars entitled "Secrets of Successful Relationships," or hear a Handel recital here—the acoustics are angelic. London lacks a real lecture circuit, but most of the arcane and/or academic societies hold their own talks for their own initiates. One such is the **Victorian Society** (tel 01871/994–1019), which often borrows the Linnean Society Lecture Room (Burlington House, Piccadilly); another is the **Theosophical Society** (tel 0171/935–9261; 50 Gloucester Place W1), whose lectures are called things like "Dreams and

Past Lives" or "Evolution and Involution: The Unfolding of Consciousness." **Rudolph Steiner House** (tel 0171/723–4400; 35 Park Rd. NW1), world center of anthroposophy, has evening workshops and talks on bridging the inner and outer worlds through creative work, and also on ecological themes, while the **London Earth Mysteries Circle** (tel 0171/916–5467; Diorama Meeting Room, 34 Osnaburgh St. NW1) goes out there, lecturing on the paranormal—"Magical and Parapsychological Aspects of Vampirism" was a recent highlight. Back in the concrete world, museums with lecture programs include the **Tate Gallery** (tel 0171/887–8000; Millbank SW1), **V&A**, and the **British Museum** (see "Late Museums," above), while the **National Film Theatre** (tel 0171/928–3232; South Bank) holds silver-screen seminars and face-to-face interviews with directors; so does the **Royal Festival Hall** (tel 0171/960–4242; South Bank Centre, South Bank E1), alongside its "Voice Box" author talks. Further out of town, the enterprising **Watermans Art Centre** (tel 0181/568–1176; High St., Brentford, Middlesex) has talks and debates on pan-artistic themes, and the beautiful **Dulwich Picture Gallery** (tel 0181/693–5254; College Rd. SE21) does Special Evening Events with wine and refreshments—a recent one had top artists and museum curators asking each other "Is Painting Still Relevant?"

Touristy, but that's O.K.... The Tower of London is closed at night, but the best deal in any case is to plan ahead and write for tickets to the **Ceremony of the Keys** (write with return materials, preferred dates, and number in party [up to 7]: The Resident Governor and Keeper of the Jewel House, Queen's House, HM Tower of London EC3; admission free). The nightly (10pm), hilarious locking-up ritual has used the same script and costumes every night for 700 years. "Halt! Who comes there?" demands the sentry. "The Keys," answers the Chief Yeoman Warder. "Whose keys?" asks the sentry. "Queen Elizabeth's keys," answers the CYW, whereupon the sentry dispenses with grammar and announces: "Pass. Queen Elizabeth's keys and all's well." Back up west, hang around **Covent Garden** and watch the buskers—everybody else does. Nearby is **Leicester Square**, home of large movie houses and a backpacker/tourist mecca, which has signs of life almost through the night. A more edifying and ancient tourist haunt, which not many know you can see at night (with a bit of queuing) is the **House of Lords** (tel 0171/219–3000; St. Margaret St. SW1; 2:30–10pm Mon–Thur; closed Easter week, May Day, July–Oct, and 3 weeks at Christmas; admission free). At the other extreme, the **Trocadero** (Coventry St. W1, Piccadilly Circus tube) has high-tech tawdry fun-house attractions, like **Qasar**, the laser-zapping game (tel 0171/734–8151), **Emaginator**, a ride simulator, and **Alien War** (tel 0171/437–2678), modeled on the film *Aliens*. All charge separate admission, which can add up to a small fortune.

Strange things to do... 18 Folgate Street (tel 0171/247–4013; 3 performances a week, 7:30–10:30pm; reservations necessary), is the meticulously authentic, early-18th-century East End home of eccentric California-born Denis Sever. He shares it with a ghostly fictional family named Jervis, and enacts a kind of philosophical *son et lumière* three nights a week, in which the audience trails several generations of invisible Jervises through the house on a time-traveling odyssey. How does London decide what to do next? It holds heated **Public Forum Debates** (Westminster Central Hall, Storey's Gate SW1; free tickets in advance from tel 0171/332–3770, Corporation of London, Guildhall, EC2), inviting politicians, community leaders, business mavens, and you. Sample titles: "Green or Gridlock? Transport in London," "2001: The Cultural Life of the Capital," and "Changing London for Good." As inside as a tourist can get.... But if you prefer schleppers and slackers to movers and shakers—and have dirty clothes—spend an unusual evening at **Duds 'n' Suds** (tel 0171/837–1122; 49–51 Brunswick Shopping Centre, Russell Sq. WC1; 8am–9pm Mon–Sat, till 6pm Sun), where you can get a cappuccino, shoot a frame of pool, lounge in armchairs, and watch cable, while doing your laundry in one of the 52 machines. Or catch an art-house movie—*My Beautiful Launderette*, perhaps—at the **Renoir** next door (tel 0171/837–8402), while the staff does the washing for you.

Ways to lose money... Gambling is perfectly legal (just witness the National Lottery), and may be about to become the best-selling tourist item if the government carries out tentative plans to reform the strange 1968 Gaming Act. As it stands, however, this is what you must do to gamble in a London casino: 1) Be over 18. 2) Go to your chosen gambling den in person. 3) Fill out a form, and show ID. A passport usually suffices, but at some places, you may have to be proposed by an existing member. 4) Wait 48 hours. This is known as the "48-hour rule." 5) Gamble. You may bring up to six guests. Alternatively: 1) Go with a member. 2) Leave with that member. While at the casino, you can expect no live entertainment, no music, no dancing, and no food at the tables, because the 1968 Gaming Act forbids a casino to "encourage or incite" gambling. A casino may serve alcohol until midnight, but not longer, since only places that offer music, dancing, food, or live entertainment can apply for an extended license. You can gamble only between 2pm and 4am, and only with chips, which you must buy with cash. You'll only find two slots per club, and their maximum payout is £250. However highly you roll, you'll never be offered a free hotel room or a credit line. If this sounds like fun, one of the top clubs anywhere is the posh, old, leather-chesterfields-and-oils **Crockford's** (tel 0171/734–0255; 30 Curzon St. W1), where you rub shoulders (or you would, if that were allowed) with international Nevada/Monte Carlo squillionaires. One of the sleaziest is the nicotine-and-bronze-mirror **Golden Horseshoe** (tel 0171/221–8788; 79 Queensway W2), where you rub shoulders with the owner of the dim sum place next door.

Coming soon... The new **Tate** will be installed in the former Bankside Power Station (opposite St. Paul's), and the British Museum will have its **Great Court**— London's largest covered square—by the millennium. Maybe the dream scheme of Queen Victoria's consort, Albert, for a cultural thoroughfare down what is now the blank Exhibition Road will also see the light of day. That idea's been dubbed **Albertopolis**. On the South Bank, near Gabriel's Wharf, the **OXO Tower** is the new hub of much art and eating, with the latest fancy restaurant packing them in for the best river view in town, and the kind of foccaccia-arugula-carambola menus Londoners expect. At the **South Bank Centre**, Richard Rogers (Paris Pompidou, London Lloyds) is slated to glaze the top with an undulating glass canopy, and generally rehash Denis Lasdun's 1960s concrete complex. Next door, if all goes to plan, the former County Hall will get an enormous **subterranean aquarium**, among the world's biggest. Above it, the long-awaited hotel plans proceed slo-o-owly. There's a vibrant **art scene** emerging in the cheaper, bigger spaces south of the river, too, most with one late-opening night a week. The 100-year-old **South London Gallery** (tel 0171/703–6120; 65 Peckham Rd.; open till 7pm Thur) could be called its hub, but check others listed in *Time Out* under "Alternative Spaces."

For adults only…Soho is one of the world's most famous red light districts, with a history of lewdness going back centuries. If you find yourself lured by one of the many unlicensed sex shows here, be warned that most are well practiced at ripping off the unwary with huge bills for colored water. **The Sunset Strip** (30 Dean St. W1, 0171/437–7229, 30 Dean St. W1, Tottenham Court Road tube stop, £10 cover), **Carnival** (tel 0171/437-8337, 12 Old Compton St. W1; Tottenham Court Road tube stop, £9 cover), and **The Raymond Revue Bar** (tel 0171/734-1593, Walkers Court W1; Piccadilly Circus tube stop, £15 cover) are the only three licensed strip shows. As for shopping, **Sh** (tel 0171/613–5458, 22 Coronet St. N1, Old Street tube stop) is a friendly little sex shop run by women for women (men are only admitted if accompanied by a woman) and **Fortunately Expectations** (tel 0171/739–0292, 75 Great Eastern Street EC2, Old Street tube stop) is nearby with a wide selection of fetish gear, clothes, toys and magazines, and they welcome everyone. In West London, **Skin Two** (0181/968–9692, 23 Grand Union Centre, Kensal Rd, W10, Ladbrooke Grove tube stop, then 23 or 52 bus) offers a good selection of fetish gear, books and magazines, as well as lots of fliers for clubs. If you're south of the river, try **Honour** (0171/401–8219, Lower Marsh St. SE1, Waterloo tube stop), which has an extensive fetish clothing range. Many of these shops present you with a featureless door and intercom, so don't be put off if you're interested in their wares.

late nigh

t dining

6

Going out to eat in
London is a nighttime
sport in its own right, not
just the necessary refueling
stop en route to some-
where else. The past few
years have been notable for

two gastronomic trends: gigantic, glamorous restaurants, and their corollary, converted pubs that serve excellent food, though there's still not much in the way of a New York–style, restaurant-anchored bar scene. London has yet to keep Spanish hours, so even in the pubs you'd better plan to eat at around 7 to 9:30. London does, however, understand the ritual of dinner like never before, and if there were an altar here for the ritual, Soho would be it.

Our listings favor those places that have extended hours, which in England means open after the pub curfew of 11pm. Restaurants that close at that hour or earlier may be included if the food's spectacular, or they have some kind of floor show, or your fellow diners are a floor show. We also have the pre-theater and happy-hour bargains covered.

The Lowdown

Big night out... If it's a glamorous dinner you're after, and money's no object, the **Ritz** is so pretty, and the waiters are properly pampering—neither does the food disappoint, though it ain't in the class of those in our Food Shrines category. Practically next door is what may be London's most glamorous, nicest, all-round best restaurant, the remarkable **Le Caprice**—which always feels celebratory. As ubiquitous as he may be, Sir Terence Conran sure knows how to draw a crowd, and his two biggest and glitziest places, **Quaglino's** and **Mezzo**, both scream "you're out on the town." You'll share your evening with suburbanites dressed to the nines, but Quag's at least has been around long enough now to earn some points for cool and a late-night clientele to match. The **Criterion**, under the aegis of big-headed, big-gobbed sur-chef Marco Pierre White (in harness with Rocco Forte), rivals the Ritz for pulchritude in its *fin-de-siècle* Byzantine fashion. It's grown up, pricey, slightly snobby, and irresistible.

Big night out, with music... The frescoed, Fellini-esque upstairs salon (downstairs is dull) at **Star of India** offers the laid-back and wonderful combination of excellent "evolved" northern Indian cuisine and Piaf numbers crooned from a grand piano. From the sublime to the ridiculous, **Gracelands Palace** is forever full of hen nights and birthdays, come to eat O.K. Chinese food and worship at the court of "the King," a.k.a. Paul Chan, owner/ Elvis impersonator of some years' standing. Less cheesy, but barely, is the fabulous flamenco show at **Costa Dorada**, the long-running late-night Spanish palace off Tottenham Court Road, where music and dancing and clapping and oléing happens twice a night. **Quaglino's** abandoned its dance floor, sadly, but still has a jazz trio on weekends from 10pm. Young sister **Mezzo**, however, seized the baton and does have dancing from 11pm to 3am, Thursday through Saturday; plus a quiet duo the rest of the week. For the classic dinner dance, the Ritz obliges on weekends, but the **Savoy** (not the Grill) does it every night except Sunday. **Simpsons-on-the-Strand** has taken to doing late jazz, too, which is odd its being so British and stuffed-shirt by nature. The music at all the above tends toward rent-a-band background noise, but for jazz you may choose to hear and London's second best pizza (**Casale Franco**'s is best), you can't beat **Pizza Express**. Choose between the serious jazz buff's Dean Street (Soho) branch, or the Sloanier, tonier Music Room at the Knightsbridge one. As for cabaret, there's only one place for your Cleo Laines, Barbara Cooks, and Bobby Shorts, and that's the **Café Royal Green Room**. This is not, repeat *not*, the Michelin-starred Café Royal Grill Room, though the food isn't at all bad. You'll be surrounded by tourists, and maybe the new breed of young lounge lizard, if it turns out that that trend sticks. If you want to see the current West End casts, the newer **Centre Stage** is close to the heart of theaterland—and to the musical breed of actor, which has clasped this supper club warmly to its bosom and likes to use up surplus post-performance energy in a song at the white baby grand.

Food shrines... Gastronomes have many choices, as long as they remember to make reservations. **Bibendum** still draws raves, even after star chef Simon Hopkinson passed the toque to Matthew Harris; it's yet another Conran shop, this one *in* the Conran Shop. Other joints that demand several days' warning before they feed you include **Aubergine** and the **River Café**, both featuring fashionable fodder, the latter in Italian. Possibly London's best chef, and one of its most lauded, the Gascon Pierre Koffman at **La Tante Claire**, is possibly also its hardest working (he's always at the stove). Three Michelin stars and terrifying prices underline his mastery. No bargain either is the suitably deep, dark, padded racing-green-and-mahogany **Le Gavroche**, which shows off the classic French cuisine of Michel Roux, son of famed Albert, (you can tell this by the dishes marked "hommage à mon père"). Nico Ladenis, who cooks at **Chez Nico** at 90 Park Lane, is the third of this triumvirate of haute French chefs. He's self-taught, though you'd never guess it. After an apprenticeship under Albert Roux's equally famous brother, Michel, then years of practice at cooking and collecting column inches, the overweening Marco Pierre White does what he does in **The Restaurant**.

Local favorites... Where to go for a reliable taste thrill, when you're not feeling culinarily snobbish, and don't want to mortgage anything? These are neighborhood places where Londoners go for great food and a comfortable evening. **The Brackenbury** is hidden in a back street in the up-and-coming restaurant row at Hammersmith, yet it's packed every night. Not only is the "new British" food here always interesting and sometimes stellar, but the atmosphere is warm and homey, the service sweet. Ditto at **St. John**, except that the vast refectory-style room is anything but cozy. The food, however, is worthy. **Bistrot Bruno** is eclipsed in fame and glamour by **l'Odeon**, where Bruno Loubet now cooks more refined versions of his robust dishes extrapolated from *cuisine de terroir,* after schooling Pierre Khodja in the style of Bruno at the old bistro. Near both is the only Chinatown restaurant that foodies don't snub, **Fung Shing**, as well as the previous incarnation of St. John, **The French House Dining Room**, with Henderson's partner Margot Clayton in charge. Much further haute fall the deservedly sold-out **Aubergine**, where Gordon Ramsay writes an enticing menu, and **Coast**, where the inventive, sometimes peculiar ideas (soup noodle of honey-roasted duck with tofu, for one) of Aussie Steven Terry don't explain why the crowds flock to an elitist and unwelcoming former car salesroom. A warmer welcome awaits at the gorgeous medium-to-high-priced—and -toned—**Criterion**. One more place—that Londoners themselves had barely discovered at press time—is the wrong-end-of-Edgware-Road **Mandalay**, the only place in London to get the cuisine of Burma. The fish dish, "melted bone hilsa," is the least expensive five-star entrée in town.

Is this a bar or a restaurant?... It's a rare phenomenon in a land of strange alcohol-licensing laws—the 11pm closing time, for starters—but a few places that claim to be restaurants are overwhelmed by their bar scenes. First up is the vast **Atlantic Bar and Grill**, the

Piccadilly Circus of late-night bars, and that's where it's located. The food has been making more of a name for itself since the early days when the bar was *it*, and nowadays ordering food is practically the only way to get in, let alone get a good, late-night table. **192** is Notting Hill's social club. It's mobbed with barflies most nights, and although the food is good, the wine list (it's officially a wine bar) is even better. Not so at the singles scene of the area, **Beach Blanket Babylon**, with its outrageous gothic-Gaudí décor and a medieval-dungeon restaurant separated by drawbridge and portcullis. In Soho central, its drunken brother, **Waxy O'Connor's**, is an equally fantastical, mad Gaelic fantasia that attempts to replicate the entire Emerald Isle indoors, with a cathedral, a street, and a forest, and is consequently jammed with backpackers. Nearby, **Bar Italia** is a coffee bar, period—no alcohol, little food, much posing—and **Café Bohème** is a bar. It does pretty decent food—just don't try eating it at 11:30pm on a Friday because you won't be able to find fork room. A few doors away, Bar Italia's offshoot, **Little Italy**, is a convenient drinking dive if you're prepared to pay the cover. In Covent Garden, **Joe Allen** has a New York–style proper bar with bar stools, as this true Manhattan transfer should, while **Maxwell's** does those sugary, blender cocktails for office workers on Fridays, and the **Palais du Jardin** has a civilized U-shaped bar for sipping wine and awaiting a table. These you wouldn't visit for the bar alone (well, maybe Maxwell's), whereas the opposite is true in tony South Kensington, at the Vietnamese **Nam Long**, whose weird alter ego, Le Shaker, serves cocktails called Yamamoto and Tramp to well-bred and well-watered locals. Nearby in Chelsea, **Kartouche** takes a cue from its wackier dishes (fillet of crocodile, coconut-caramel-yam cake) and goes wild and free late at night, with an actual nightclub in the basement for overflow.

Is this a pub or a restaurant?... The single most noticeable change in nighttime London is the proliferation of pubs converted to casual restaurants serving real food—no ploughman's lunches, no oozy lasagna, no pink prepacked pork pies. One of the first was the Camden **Crown & Goose**, which was popular from the time it installed the first sofa, but is now off the scale, thanks to the neighborhood's groove resurgence. Not far away is the **Engineer**, which is far less frenetic, a bit older, with a garden, and really good char-grilled, Mid-Eastern-dip, focaccia-type food. Near to that are the big windows, big pastas, and family atmosphere of **The Lansdowne**. Northeast in Islington, the *craic* is loud at the venerable **Minogues**, where the restaurant is mercifully separate from the stocious Murphy's drinkers, and at **Filthy McNasty's**, where the food isn't quite that bad, but the drinking is nevertheless paramount. **The Eagle** was actually the very first hardwood-floored foodie pub of all, and still serves great rustic Italian fodder to crowds. But West London takes the biscuit for perfecting the foodie pub. In the hip environs of Portobello, there are three in close proximity: **The Cow** and **The Westbourne** practically face each other, creating a summertime Woodstock scene on the (thoughtfully extended) sidewalks, and attracting slightly different breeds (see The Bar Scene). Food-wise, The Cow has a crustacean fetish (as you'd expect from a Conran—owner Tom is one of Sir T's sons), and great Irish soda bread, while The Westbourne is more Mediterranean—grilled veggies, onion tart, etc. Third, there's the **Prince Bonaparte**, which usually gets accused of having the best chalkboard menu and the best puddings. In Kensington, there's **The Abingdon**, which is indistinguishable from a restaurant, and, further south, a pair of siblings which bear scant resemblance to the pubs they once were, and which attract sport-jacket types who give the local boozer a very wide berth. Prices are not low, but neither is food quality, at **The Enterprise** and **The** (aptly named) **Establishment**. It's a toss-up whether the Notting Hill Gate **Windsor Castle** is better for the garden in summer or for the tiny, cozy, wood-paneled rooms with log fires in winter; the food's British and there are oysters. Finally, Maida Vale's Warrington Hotel is a gorgeous Art Nouveau palais with a terrible identity crisis— **Ben's Thai**, a full-blown Thai kitchen, is secreted upstairs.

Pre-theater cheapies... When you splurged your food budget on orchestra seats for some West End musical or a box at the Coliseum, what better than **Wagamama** for fast-fueling before curtain-up? It closes too early for after-theater eats. Across the Covent Garden Piazza, a bargain, speed-delivered (6–7pm) pre-theater deal is offered at that toniest of American places, **Christopher's**, while another part of this neighborhood houses the mad monks of **Belgo Centraal** who'll fill you fast with *moules-frites* for a tenner. Really cheap, but with nil style, are the nevertheless useful St. Martins Lane branches of the chains **Pret à Manger** and **Café Flo**, while the unique **Alfred** offers guileful Formica that's only pretending to be style-free, and a pre-theater bargain British menu whose glazed knuckle of bacon and sticky toffee pudding will definitely see you through to the final curtain call. Ditto **Rules**, where the perfectly classic English food is on sale from 5 to 6pm, and **Simpson's-in-the-Strand**, whose two-courses-for-ten-quid is offered a half hour later. A little further off in St. James's, **Quaglino's** also does a 5:30 to 6:30 pre-curtain deal, while in the beating heart of theaterland, nearly next door to the Misérables, is the best of the cheap Italian restaurants, **Centrale**.

After the applause... Repair immediately to where the actors go in London as in New York, **Joe Allen**, or where the leads, director and playwright go, **The Ivy**—as long as you remembered to reserve. If you didn't, the other side of Charing Cross Road has several options that will feed you late at night: **Soho Soho**, where the first- (ground) floor rotisserie is perennially loud and full, and **Café Bohème**, if you can squeeze in past the crowds of drinkers, are both French-ish, while the-biggest-joint-in-Europe, **Mezzo**, must surely be able to squeeze you in— certainly in the Mezzonine, upstairs—and it's open later than anywhere. Anywhere except **Little Italy** and the **Atlantic**, that is, where if it's late in the week, you'll probably not get in. From the Atlantic's velvet rope you can practically spit at wonderfully fusty **Bentley's**, where the first-floor Oyster Bar's happy hour usefully starts at 10:30pm. Otherwise, aim for some swift salt-baked chicken at **Fung Shing** or a platter of deer at **Rules**, both taking orders till 11:30. If you get too hungry for dinner at 10, hit the **Savoy Grill** for its two-part before-and-after-theater supper. And if you don't want to wind down yet, see which Lloyd Webber warblers are at **Centre Stage** tonight (as long as it's Thursday or the weekend).

Off–West End eating... The Islington Almeida has the divine, upscale pizzas of **Casale Franco** in a hidden courtyard nearby, though be warned that you're not allowed to order only pizza, and there's no booking, so come *very* early to make the play on time, or queue after. If you caught the show at the Gate Theatre, the nearest places to eat are **Kensington Place**, and that cute pub, the **Windsor Castle** (last food orders by 10:30). Not far from there, one of London's loveliest, little-known summertime dinner-and-show combos is the opera, or whatever, at Holland Park Open Air Theatre, and supper at **The Belvedere**, preferably at one of the seven terrace tables. The obvious place for anywhere South Bank—from the Olivier to the Purcell Room, and movies at the National Film Theatre, too—is the **People's Palace**, although the way to miss the crush is to eat there during the performance. Unless you've left it too late, avoid the **Archduke**, which doesn't deserve its South Bank crowd-by-default. Around the Barbican it's still a shameful culinary desert, except for the buzzing Clerkenwell enclave, where you'll find **St. John** for ambiance and great food—a five- to ten-minute stroll, but get directions. Over in Hammersmith, the obvious post-Riverside or -Lyric target is the **Brackenbury**, though you won't be the only one with that idea. The **River Café**, though sharing a post code, is not near, and is too dear and special to share the billing with a play.

Offstage stars... It helps to watch a little British TV before attempting to celebrity-spot in this town. This ain't no L.A. Movie folk and—especially—rock people do visit, though, and seem to feel at home among the leafier parts of town, generally toward the west. **Room at the Halcyon** in Holland Park harbors many a local celeb, some of whom have fame that has spread further than Dover: John Cleese, for instance, and Sting, and Elton John. Next door, in groovy Notting Hill, **192** hosts fashion designers, writers, and anyone with the last name Freud (author Esther, sister designer Bella, and father Lucien) or Conran (Jasper the designer, Shirley the schlock novelist, not Terence the patriarch), although many will have defected to Tom Conran's **The Cow**, around the corner. **Daphne's** hosts glitzy ladies of the Ivana ilk, and **Le Caprice** and **The Ivy** are magnetic to movers-and-shakers in the worlds of architecture, business, art dealing, publishing—you name it. The latter is

LONDON ⟨ LATE NIGHT DINING

also a thespian haunt, being in theaterland, a tonier choice than the perennial **Joe Allen**, the collective green room for the West End. If only you knew what they looked like, you'd spot homegrown politicians and big-time newspaper editors and columnists at **The Savoy Grill**, while anyone writing for the *Guardian* goes to **St. John**, along with architects. **Wódka** is the secret hangout of Jerry Hall and Charles Saatchi, to name two utterly unrelated sometime-regulars, plus *Evening Standard* hacks, Eurotrash, and fashion-biz creatures. The **Atlantic** is the central posing palace, thanks to its late drinking license, and ever-more-stringently snotty door policy, but *everyone* is spotted sooner or later getting a late-night caffeine fix at **Bar Italia**.

Trysting places... The **Belvedere** has one of the most gorgeous London locations, secreted right inside Holland Park, though winter amour would flourish faster at the delicious and decadent **Le Caprice**, with its moderne black and silver and its well-spaced, white-dressed tables. It always pampers, regardless of your purpose. Sister **The Ivy** is hopeless for romance, being one of the noisiest table-hopping locations in town. There's something illicit about Soho's **French House Dining Room**, hidden above the notorious, ever-crammed pub with its photos of French boxers, lined with mirrors, and seats upholstered in vermillion. It's the earlier success of the St. John duo, so the food's great, too, in a hearty, naked way. **Rules** has been serving deer and grouse to the gentry and the hoi polloi for two centuries, and can lavish a table with flattering nannylike attention, while staff at **The Savoy Grill**, used to Captains of Industry and Barons of Print, are the most discreet in London. Both the **Ritz** and the **Criterion** provide vast and achingly beautiful frames for your love story.

Caveat emptor... The places you've heard are the best this or that—are they really so hot? Let's see...there's **Coast**, which is strictly for posing, unless you like paying over the odds for odd food, and there's **Vong**, sibling of NYC star Jean-Georges Vongerichten's NYC star, Vong. London's most-read reviewer named Vong "Restaurant of the Year" five minutes after the opening, but does a (stunningly bland) appetizer called "27 Vegetables Simmered in Their Own Juices and Spices" belong in down-to-earth London? Or spoon-feeding service by obsequious silk-vested French waiters? You make the call. Vong does Thai-Alsatian, but other cuisines have their day in the sun, like the Indian *Balti*. Supposedly from a remote region of Pakistan, but actually from Birmingham (up north), this gloppy spiced meat scooped out of an iron *karahi* with nan bread is the emperor's new curry–it can taste nice, but it's overpriced and unauthentic.

Late... In this town, late still means after pub closing, or 11pm, though for restaurants, with their slightly more liberal licensing laws, curfew is often extended to midnight. The following are the only (legal and nonmembership) places in London that will feed you after the clock strikes twelve: **Atlantic, Costa Dorada, Centre Stage, Joe Allen, Little Italy, Vingt-Quatre, Quaglino's, Simpsons-in-the-Strand, Mezzo, Soho Soho, Bistrot 190, Coast, the Atlantic, Belgo Centraal,** and **Café Bohème**.

Late late late... Twenty-four-hour restaurants? Ha ha ha. No, really, there are four: **Bar Italia**, if you don't mind standing, and dining on panetone and gelato; **Brick Lane Beigel Bake**, if you don't mind standing, and dining on bagels with margarine; **Harry's Bar**, a.k.a. the "British breakfast," if you don't mind sharing with transvestite groovers and dining on a fry-up (a.k.a. the British breakfast); and **Vingt-Quatre**, if you don't mind sharing with trust-funded Eurotrash in Fulham. There are also two execrable places that every London teenager knows: the three-floored, fluorescent-lit Chinatown **Lido** and the King's Road burger dive **Up All Night**. Look them up in the phone book if you're desperate.

The Index

£££££	more than £40
££££	£25–£40
£££	£18–£25
££	£10–£18
£	less than £10

Per person for three courses and coffee, no wine.

The Abingdon. The least publike of the multitudinous pub-into-restaurant conversions, this has a railway carriage of a back room with private red booths, and a chef who won a Michelin star while at a different restaurant. Here he does chicken liver and foie gras parfait, as well as the most intense and freshest sorbets in London.... *Tel 0171/937–3339. 54 Abingdon Rd. W8, High Street Kensington tube stop. ££*

Alfred. Good British grub in a high-school lunch hall from the fifties, where the beer list is better than the one for wine. You might eat smoked haddock, poached egg and cress salad, glazed knuckle of bacon with pickled cabbage and pease pudding, and burnt cream. It's near but not in theaterland.... *Tel 0171/240–2566. 245 Shaftsbury Ave. WC2, Tottenham Court Road tube stop. Reservations recommended for dinner. £££*

Archduke. A wine bar in a converted brick-walled warehouse, whose main attraction is its proximity to the South Bank Centre and its otherwise sad catering options. Stand in line downstairs for quiches, pâtés, salads, soups, or go up to the restaurant for a large variety of sausages. The food's only O.K., the atmosphere—especially when there's live jazz—can be good.... *Tel 0171/928–9370. Concert Hall Approach, South Bank SE1, Waterloo tube stop. Reservations recommended for dinner. ££*

Atlantic Bar & Grill. Emphasis is on the bar side of this anomaly in the licensing laws that looks like a jazzed-up, parquet-floored ocean liner. Despite being the size of a small village, it gets packed out most nights, and weekends are a zoo. Some food's good—Mediterranean or Asian appetizer platters; linguini with cashew-cilantro pesto.... *Tel 0171/ 734–4888. 20 Glasshouse St. W1, Piccadilly Circus tube stop. Reservations recommended on weekends. DC not accepted. £££*

Aubergine. A raving success since its opening year (1994), this small, Provençal-looking foodie haunt in Chelsea has an inventive Franglais menu (literally—viz: "sea bass with jus vanille"; "pan-fried red mullet, sauce épices, pommes frites"), the work of young Scottish star Gordon Ramsay (who also happens to be an ex-pro-footballer).... *Tel 0171/ 352–3449. 11 Park Walk SW10, Sloane Square tube stop. Reservations recommended. ££££*

Bar Italia. This Soho institution is the ur-espresso bar, always open, (nearly) always full of life, and lined with Rocky Marciano-abilia. Sandwiches, panetone, and unmemorable gelati are the meager food choices, but the espresso and cappuccino are the business.... *Tel 0171/437–4520. 22 Frith St. W1, Leicester Square tube stop. Reservations not accepted. No credit cards. £*

Beach Blanket Babylon. This outrageous-looking Gaudì-in-a-dungeon fantasy is the nearest thing to a singles bar you'll find in hip Notting Hill. Cross the drawbridge to the restaurant to pick up a meal here, too—glass noodle and crab salad with sweet chili dressing; duck with gnocchi & ceps.... *Tel 0171/229–2907. 45 Ledbury Rd. W11, Notting Hill Gate tube stop. Reservations recommended for dinner. AE, DC not accepted. ££–£££*

Belgo Centraal. The Belgian-style (a contradiction in terms, we used to think) faux refectory, where you can order mussels and fries, *waterzooi* (fish stew), and cherry beer from waiters dressed as Mad Max monks, in a steel, concrete, and pine basement, entered via elevator. There's an older brother in Camden, **Belgo Noord**.... *Tel 0171/813–2233. 50 South Earlham St. WC2, Covent Garden tube stop. Reservations recommended. DC not accepted. ££*

Belvedere. A beautiful midpark setting for this serene room of huge windows and white linens far outstrips the Med-Brit menu (blackened tuna; confit of duck, garlic mash; welsh rarebit; chocolate marquise).... *Tel 0171/602–1238. Holland Park, Abbotsbury Rd. W8, Holland Park tube stop. Reservations recommended. ££££*

Ben's Thai. A big off-the-beaten-track Art Nouveau pub harbors this wood-paneled dining room upstairs. There's better Thai food in town, but value and casual ambiance this has got.... *Tel 0171/266–3134. The Warrington Hotel, 93 Warrington Crescent W9, Warwick Avenue tube stop. Reservations recommended for dinner. AE, DC not accepted. ££*

Bentley's. Venerable fishy corner of the West End that style forgot—which makes it worth seeking out, especially after 10:30, when there's a (food) happy hour in the Oyster Bar.... *Tel 0171/734–4756. 11–15 Swallow St. W1, Piccadilly Circus tube stop. ££–££££*

Bibendum. The replacement of Simon Hopkinson by his protegé Matthew Harris has not harmed this cherished Brit-accented French treat beneath the stained-glass windows of the Michelin tire man (this was that company's HQ).... *Tel 0171/581–5817. Michelin House, 81 Fulham Rd. SW3, South Kensington tube stop. Reservations recommended. DC not accepted. £££££*

Bistrot 190. This is the original of ubiquitous Antony Worrall Thompson's (hereafter AWT) several Med-style cool and casual places. Near the big South Ken museums, it's got a permanent well-heeled crowd feasting on big food that lists every ingredient: e.g., pork chop with rhubarb compote and cheese-and-mustard mash. The lemon tart here is the sine qua non.... *Tel 0171/581–5666. 190 Queensgate SW7, South Kensington tube stop. Reservations not accepted. £££*

Bistrot Bruno. Bruno Loubet, with his organ meats and peasant cooking techniques (in, say, neck of lamb and tripe-stuffed potato) that other chefs eschew, his swoon-inducing onion tarte tatin and chocolate-enrobed sorbets, has moved to his new place, l'Odeon, leaving this little find in the capable hands of his longtime collaborator, Pierre Khodja.... *Tel 0171/734–4545. 63 Frith St. W1, Leicester Square tube stop. Reservations recommended. £££*

Brackenbury. Get a cab to this peach-colored peach in a secret Hammersmith pocket, and roll around in the vivid fun food of young chefs Adam and Katie Robinson. A mixed plate of all the fishy appetizers is always on; otherwise, market availability dictates—saffron turbot and mussel stew, onion-thyme tart, sautéed brains, a burger, blood-orange sorbet. It's loud and friendly.... *Tel 0181/748–0107. 129 Brackenbury Rd. W6, Hammersmith tube stop. Reservations recommended. ££*

Brick Lane Beigel Bake. An East End institution, this 24-hour boil-then-bakery offers standing room only for noshing on filled bagels and filthy coffee at giveaway rates.... *Tel 0171/ 729–0616. 159 Brick Lane E1, Whitechapel tube stop. No credit cards. £*

Café Bohème. More useful as a Soho rendezvous and after-hours drinking den (as your bruised elbows will notice) than as a restaurant, this continental brasserie nevertheless has perfectly fine food, along the ciabatta (a focaccia-like bread)-roast veg-goat's cheese-sandwich axis.... *Tel 0171/734–0623. 13 Old Compton St. W1, Leicester Square tube stop. Reservations recommended for dinner. DC not accepted. ££*

Café Flo. The best of the nearly identical Parisian wannabes, this—and its branches—does a good, fast, cheap soup-or-salad, steak-or-fish-with-fries deal. Many other dishes from cassoulet to goat's cheese salad are augmented by the occasional regional wine and food promotion.... *Tel 0171/ 836–8289. 51 St. Martin's Lane WC2, Charing Cross tube stop. DC not accepted. £–££*

Café Royal. The Grill Room's got famous food, while the Green Room's got one of London's two true cabaret stages, with more-than-O.K. menus with the song stylings. The big names of the circuit get booked in here, amid the plush and gilt.... *Tel 0171/437–9090. 68 Regent St. W1, Piccadilly Circus tube stop. Reservations recommended. £££££*

Le Caprice. It has been a wonderful experience to spend time here since the old London fave was reopened by the classy Corbin-King duo (see also **The Ivy**). Shiny eighties-black, sparkly lighting, Japanesey flowers, starched white cloths contain a round-the-world menu (bisque of Dublin Bay prawns; champagne risotto with Perigord truffles; deep-fried cod & chips). Service is perfect.... *Tel 0171/ 629–2239.*

Arlington House, Arlington St. SW1, Green Park tube stop. Reservations recommended. ££££

Casale Franco. Ask, or you'll never find the cobbled courtyard entrance (with hotly contested summer tables) to this Islington staple. Famous for great pizza, it has an arrogant no-pizza-only policy, no booking, and a sometimes surly staff, but the brick-walled warehouse-chic, and the compulsory other food (calf's liver, cuttlefish in its ink, polenta, salads) is fine.... *Tel 0171/226–8994. Behind 134 Upper St. N1, Highbury and Islington tube stop. Reservations not accepted. AE, DC not accepted. ££–£££*

Centrale. A lovely, spartan little café in centrale theaterland, where the pastas are the business—as is the *zuppa pavese* (chicken soup with egg) and homemade gnocchi. However, all big cheap, hot and fresh dishes must be consumed before 10pm, with your own wine, if you choose... *Tel 0171/437–5513. 16 Moor St. W1. Reservations not accepted. No credit cards. Leicester Square tube stop. £*

Centre Stage. The Mountbatten Hotel had the good idea of cashing in on its Covent Garden theaterland location and opening this late-night supper club. Now, hyped-up performers from every musical in town drop by to extend the limelight.... *Tel 0171/379–6009. Seven Dials, Monmouth St. WC2, Covent Garden tube stop. Reservations recommended. Open Thur–Sat 10pm–1am. ££££*

Chez Nico at Ninety Park Lane. Nico Ladenis, self-taught superstar of London cuisine, has a lower profile than he used to, maybe because he's finally settled down in the patrician salon he deserves. Here are well-padded seats and patrons, obsequious service, and complicated perfection on the plate, replete with foie gras.... *Tel 0171/409–1290. Grosvenor House, 90 Park Lane W1, Marble Arch tube stop. Reservations recommended. Dress smart. £££££*

Christopher's. The diametric opposite of the above, this is upscale U.S. East Coast dining transplanted, uncut, to Covent Garden. Up the stone staircase is a soaring mirrored space, with plain broiled steak, chicken and fish, fries, creamed spinach, and nutmeggy mash on offer. Below is a café that halves the check. Brunch is the best.... *Tel 0171/*

240–4222. 18 Wellington St. WC2, Covent Garden tube stop. Reservations recommended. ££ (café, brunch), ££££ (restaurant)

Coast. A cool (as in cold shoulder) showroom for moneyed types. Ceiling lights that look like plaster breasts, and a computer-drawn wall-sized artwork that reproduces itself on your check, then erases itself every night, go with wacky Thai/Middle Eastern-Mediterranean/French food—corn-fed chicken, parmesan-and-corn croquettes, haricot vert (sic), jus of sariette.... *Tel 0171/495–5999. 26 Albermarle St. W1, Green Park tube stop. Reservations recommended. ££££*

Costa Dorada. A frenetic Spanish dive that's always been there; best late at night with as many people as you can drag in. The beautifully hokey flamenco shows (twice nightly, around 9pm and midnight) are far better than the food, but you'll be O.K. with simple stuff like tortilla and tapas.... *Tel 0171/636–7139. 47–55 Hanway Place W1, Tottenham Court Road tube stop. Reservations recommended on weekends. ££–££££*

The Cow. Tom Conran's cute, wood-paneled pub conversion manages to evoke both a living room on the Liffey and one of his dad's (Sir Terence's) super-restaurants, while hordes of hip Notting Hillbillies spill all over the sidewalk in summer (see also **The Westbourne**). Food's simple seafood, soda bread and butter, soups, and Irish stew; upstairs is a more formal dining room.... *Tel 0171/221–0021. 89 Westbourne Park Rd. W2, Westbourne Park tube stop. Reservations recommended upstairs. AE, DC not accepted. £–£££*

The Criterion. Marco Pierre White joined egos with Rocco Forte late in 1995 to liven up this heaven-to-behold gold mosaic-tiled Byzantine hall with a spiffy French-esque menu, executed by a pair of head chefs for a clientele used to exercising its taste buds at all the best places. Roast leg of rabbit stuffed with calamari, and pearl-barley risotto are winter dishes you may find; the lemon tarte is among the best there is.... *Tel 0171/930–2626. 224 Piccadilly W1, Piccadilly Circus tube stop. Reservations recommended. £££*

Crown & Goose. It was the second pub to be also a restaurant (after the Eagle), and retains its squashy sofas, sidewalk tables, steak sandwich with Dijon mayo, risotto, and stuffed mushrooms, even though it can't really take the pressure of the multitudes in search of the Camden thrill.... *Tel 0171/ 485–2342. 100 Arlington Rd. NW1, Camden Town tube stop. Reservations not accepted. No credit cards. £*

Daphne's. Where the lady lunches; big hair and gilt buttons are de rigueur after dark, when your baubles should be real. Food from the Mediterranean hit parade (fritto misto, sea bass baked with fennel, an unctuous Caesar, shellfish and risotti) is completely beside the point, but it does matter in which flagstone-floored conservatory you sit—don't settle for the middle.... *Tel 0171/589–4257. 112 Draycott Ave. SW3, South Kensington tube stop. Reservations recommended. ££££*

The Eagle. The first, the very first, of the pub conversions for food-centric people that are now everywhere, and it's still one of the best—as proven by the impossibility getting to sit down for your Tuscan pork loin roast with garlic, fennel, and roast potatoes, or perennial *bife Ana* (sandwich of marinated steak). As with all these places, cigarette fallout can quarrel with the aroma of food.... *Tel 0171/837–1353. 159 Farringdon Rd. EC1, Farringdon tube stop. No credit cards. ££*

The Engineer. In a quiet and pretty backwater where Camden becomes Primrose Hill, this restaurant-in-a-pub co-run by Sir Laurence Olivier's daughter, Tamsin, has bookable tables and waiter service, a Med-style menu of soups and salads, grilled meat, fish, and vegetables, and a garden.... *Tel 0171/ 722–0950. 65 Gloucester Ave. NW1, Camden Town tube stop. AE, DC not accepted. ££*

The Enterprise. The poshest pub you'll ever see (apart from its sister, **The Establishment**) with perfectly adequate, but not too exciting food—lentil soup, lemon sole—and table service. Dress as if this were a restaurant and try to spot the difference.... *Tel 0171/584–3148. 35 Walton St. SW3, Knightsbridge tube stop. DC not accepted. £££*

The Establishment. Self-consciously wacky décor has ocher walls and *objets* of Aboriginal descent in yet another pub conversion, with food in the grilled-meat-and-fish vein. Loud groups of posh youth like it here.... *Tel 0171/589– 7969. 1 Gloucester Rd. SW7, Gloucester Road tube stop. DC not accepted. £££*

Filthy McNasty's. Named after a legendary unwashed Irishman—or more likely, after a marketing meeting—this Islington dive is not notable for its kitchen, though there is one. Hilariously, the management's dubbed it Hell's Kitchen. It serves stew.... *Tel 0171/837–6067. 68 Amwell St. EC1, Angel tube stop. No credit cards. £*

French House Dining Room. Above the Soho pub of the same name is a tiny cozy dining salon, all red banquettes and mirrors, where Fergus Henderson and Margot Clayton of St. John honed their craft, and which still does their kind of Scottish-French nursery food—crab and mayonnaise, garlicky salads, giant lamb shanks, homemade cake and ice cream.... *Tel 0171/437–2477. 49 Dean St. W1, Leicester Square tube stop. Reservations recommended. ££–£££*

Fung Shing. London's Chinatown, though improving, is not a patch on New York's or San Francisco's, but this cool green place has dishes like salt-baked chicken; fried intestines; stewed duck with yam available even to those who can't decipher pictograms.... *Tel 0171/437–1539. 15 Lisle St. WC2, Leicester Square tube stop. Reservations recommended for dinner. £££*

Le Gavroche. A very well-known center of gastroporn, especially since the Roux brother *patrons* are the Julia Children of the U.K. Son of Albert, Michel Roux, wears the toque in the dark-green subterranean boîte, keeping the family recipes warm, and adding his own. These are welded to the highest classical tradition, littered with foie gras, truffles, and lobster, but certified best of breed.... *Tel 0171/408–0881. 43 Upper Brook St. W1, Marble Arch tube stop. Reservations recommended. Jacket and tie required. £££££*

Gracelands Palace. Paul Chan is the only Chinese restaurateur to perform Elvis impersonations. His place is not famous for food, so make sure you're booking a show night.... *Tel 0171/639–3961. 881 Old Kent Rd. SE15, Elephant & Castle tube, then bus 53, 172, or 173. Reservations recommended. AE not accepted. £–££*

The Ivy. There is nothing wrong with The Ivy: no nastiness toward nobodies; lots of food you want to eat (very eclectic here—blinis and caviar to shepherd's pie, and irresistible Desserts R Us); and nearly every night, a glamorous feeling that you're in the place where things happen.... *Tel 0171/836–4751. 1 West St. WC2, Leicester Square tube stop. Reservations recommended. ££££*

Joe Allen. You could be on New York's 46th Street, from the brick walls to the corn muffin with the broiled chicken breast and salsa; from the cobb salad and warm banana bread with caramel sauce to the theatrical flock after curtain calls.... *Tel 0171/836–0651. 13 Exeter St. WC2, Covent Garden tube stop. No credit cards. £££*

Kartouche. Scene of scenes for Chelsea girls and boys, pop music types, models and their coke dealers, where a no-booking-for-dinner policy guarantees a full bar. When you eventually get dinner, it's good and slightly trippy—roasted garlic and hummus; Cajun salmon with fried banana; Mars Bar spring roll.... *Tel 0171/823–3515. 329–331 Fulham Rd. SW10, Fulham Broadway tube stop. DC not accepted. £££*

Kensington Place. Chef Rowley Leigh has been flavor of the month, but has settled into being just hugely liked by the legion of table-hopping regulars who call this glass-walled echo chamber "KP". Grilled foie gras on sweet-corn blini is Leigh's signature appetizer; baked tamarillo with vanilla ice cream the dessert; in between, maybe rabbit merguez with harissa (Moroccan spicy sausage; hot sauce).... *Tel 0171/727–3184. 201 Kensington Church St. W8, Notting Hill Gate tube stop. Reservations recommended. AE, DC not accepted. £££*

The Lansdowne. This example of the pub-resto (presto? respub?) genre, steps away from the Engineer, is nicest in summer, when light streams through the French windows, and you can nab a sidewalk table to consume the garlicky pasta salads and fruity puddings they do so well. In winter, hot soups and stews and big squashy couches suffice.... *Tel 0171/483–0409. 90 Gloucester Ave. NW1, Chalk Farm tube stop. No credit cards. ££*

Little Italy. Doors away from Bar Italia is this Italian diner that the same Polledri family opened in early '96. It's not notable in the menu department—grilled tuna and vegetables, sundry pastas—nor for its stark décor, but its opening hours are beautiful: until 4am for food and 3am for drinks, though a cover's charged for cocktails alone.... *Tel 0171/ 734–4737. 21 Frith St. W1, Leicester Square tube stop. Reservations not accepted. ££*

Mandalay. Marvelous Burmese menus are smilingly explained by the two brothers who run their place with love, and Mom may emerge from the kitchen, too. You'll need footnotes, because Burmese is not a cuisine in the average omnivore's canon, and even dishes that sound boring (shrimp fritters; chicken papaya salad) aren't. Don't miss "melted bone hilsa".... *Tel 0171/258–3696. 444 Edgware Road. W2, Edgware Road tube stop. AE not accepted. ££*

Maxwell's. This place practically introduced the all-beef patty with correct fixings to London nearly a quarter century ago. See the mural of Martin Luther King, Mick Jagger, Queen Elizabeth, and others sharing lurid cocktails; avoid the Reuben.... *Tel 0171/836–0303. 8–9 James St. WC2, Covent Garden tube stop. DC not accepted. ££*

Mezzo. The biggest restaurant in Europe! Rah! Rah! How did we ever live without Sir Terence opening a new bigger, brighter, louder, later place every year? This 700-cover behemoth stands on the ghost of the old Marquee Club, where rock and punk were born, and is split into three—the café/patis-serie, the no-booking upstairs Mezzonine (red duck curry; chicken and coconut salad), and the open-kitchen main salon downstairs (crab mayonnaise; bone marrow and parmesan; fig tart). Glitz and glam and G&Ts for suburban-ites.... *Tel 0171/314–4000. 100 Wardour St. W1V, Leicester Square tube stop. ££–££££*

Minogues. Islington's Irish outpost is best when it's most rowdy, though the semi-separate brasserie side of the operation is nice for a Sunday brunch of Irish stew and colcannon, or oys-ters and soda bread, and a pint of Murphy's, of course.... *Tel 0171/354–4440. 80 Liverpool Rd. N1, Angel tube stop. ££*

Nam Long. The quite ridiculous concept of marrying a Vietnam-ese restaurant (which calls summer rolls "crystal spring rolls") to a singles-heavy bar called Le Shaker (which serves "golden classic and exotic cocktails") works very well, judg-ing by the crowds. Must be the tropical fish in the glass pil-lars downstairs.... *Tel 0171/373–1926. 159 Old Brompton Rd. SW5, Gloucester Road tube stop. £££*

L'Odeon. Bruno Loubet's (of Bistrot Bruno) 200-seater La Coupole of the West End is a *vrai* brasserie serving jellied eel with cauliflower cream and steak frites; foie gras with roast pears and sticky puddings. The strange shape of the long, low-ceilinged room is only made stranger by fabric screen partitioning, but get one of the arched-windows-over-Regent-Street tables and you won't notice. The food's the real fun here, though.... *Tel 0171/287–1400. 65 Regent St. W1, Piccadilly Circus tube stop. £££*

192. A never-ending trend in Notting Hillbilly circles, this color-washed wine bar-resto has a long and interesting wine list, fashionable salad ingredients (gremolata, Jerusalem artichokes), appetizers that are more enticing than entrées, and a high-decibel crush of cuties hurling gossip at each other.... *Tel 0171/229–0482. 192 Kensington Park Rd. W11, Ladbroke Grove tube stop. Reservations recommended. ££–£££*

Palais du Jardin. Wooden-floored, halogen spotlit, this big brasserie is forever full because it's priced a notch below what it's worth. Volume can mar the service, and bits of the large and likeably hokey menu (coq au vin; fish soup; fricassee of lobster and chicken) don't work, but there's always the shellfish stand.... *Tel 0171/379–5353. 136 Long Acre, WC2, Covent Garden tube stop. Reservations recommended. ££*

The People's Palace. Run independently (by the well-known family of hoteliers, the Levins) from the Royal Festival Hall, with menus by TV chef Gary Rhodes, this bargain has the best river view in all London, so reserve a window table. Some food's lovely (snail-and-mushroom papardelle; lemon-crumbed cod with anchovy dressing), some less so (a greaseball goat's cheese risotto), and service verges on the peculiar, but let's count our blessings, eh? The South Bank needed a place like this.... *Tel 0171/928–9999. Level 3, Royal Festival Hall, South Bank Centre SE1, Waterloo tube stop. Reservations recommended. ££*

Pizza Express. London's favorite chain serves thin-crusted, always-good pies with no surprises on top, and this branch becomes a major jazz venue most evenings. Nothing else on the menu is worth eating.... *Tel 0171/437–9595. 10 Dean St. W1, Tottenham Court Road tube stop. £–£££ (cover), ££ (food)*

Pret à Manger. A fast-food chain you'll see around, that prides itself on the above-average sandwich (chicken tikka, cucumber, mint mayo on granary bread; goat's cheese salad on walnut-raisin; cheddar-and-mushroom croissant), plus good salads and cakes and pretty awful sushi and espresso. This one lets you sit and is open till 11pm.... *Tel 0171/379–5335. 77 St. Martin's Lane WC2, Charing Cross tube stop. No credit cards. £*

Prince Bonaparte. Oh, not *another* pub-restaurant, surely? Yes, another, and round the corner from The Cow and the Westbourne, too, but the daily changing menus are especially inventive here, and the room's especially big. Grab the fish cakes if they're on, and save room for fab British puddings, like pear crumble with custard.... *Tel 0171/229–5912. 80 Chepstow Rd. W2, Notting Hill Gate tube stop. ££–£££*

Quaglino's. Quag's was the watchword for a big night on the town in the twenties, then Conran resurrected it, and all London talked about it again. The first flush is past, but you still feel like you're being filmed when you sashay down the sweeping stair into this ocean liner of a restaurant, with its sequoia-sized, artist-daubed pillars, "crustacea altar," and soaring ceiling. Most of the food's just fine too—saffron crab tart; rosemary-crusted rabbit with polenta; good puddings.... *Tel 0171/930–6767. 16 Bury St. SW1, Green Park tube stop. Reservations recommended. £££*

The Restaurant. The place that loves itself. When the chef is in, excitement flickers uncoolly around the serious, deep-carpeted, all-but-soundproof room, because the chef, Marco Pierre White, is all charisma and fame. His cuisine is based on what he learned *chez* his mentor, Michel Roux (Le Gavroche), but has gone stellar on its own. Signature dishes include his version of (La Tante Claire) Pierre Koffman's signature dish of pig's trotter stuffed with sweetbreads and wild mushrooms, and a pear tarte tatin.... *Tel 0171/259–5380. Hyde Park Hotel, 66 Knightsbridge SW1, Knightsbridge tube stop. Reservations recommended. £££££*

The Ritz. The rococo Louis XVI, bemirrored, bemuraled room is heartrendingly beautiful, overlooking the hotel's formal Italian Garden by day, lit rosily to flatter by night. Order apt Crab Antoinette—an artist's impression of shellfish salad, with only the best crustacean parts, which is (like most everything on the menu) exquisite, and royally rich. Chefs have come and gone a lot, and so has the quality, but it's settled down now, and the food, too, is a treat with a warranty.... *Tel 0171/493–8181. Piccadilly W1, Green Park tube stop. Reservations recommended. Jacket and tie required; no jeans. £££££*

River Café. This exceptional uber-Italian salon began life as the staff canteen for Richard Rogers' architectural practice, run by his wife, Ruth, and her pal, Rose Grey. They still run it, but it's long been the style-setting place to go for the city slicker's version of rustic regional meals.... *Tel 0171/381–8824. Thames Wharf, Rainville Rd. W6, Hammersmith tube stop, and bus 11. Reservations recommended. AE, DC not accepted. ££££*

Room at the Halcyon. A very young chef presides over this conservatory-like unhotelly room, with straitjacketed chairs (you know, those tie-on covers), and the wall-art food is fresh (sesame tuiles with seared scallop, wasabi, and marinated cucumber); desserts (banana pancakes with butterscotch sauce) are wicked; vegetarians are honored with an entire menu.... *Tel 0171/221–5411. 129 Holland Park Ave. W11, Holland Park tube stop. £££–££££*

Rules. London's oldest restaurant looks Edwardian, though it was founded in the Georgian age and renovated a moment ago. Most diners are, predictably, doing business, or else are on the sort of tourist trail which likes to tick things off on lists, and counts being served (pretty good) "deer" (that's venison) from Rules's Scottish estate by waiters in long white aprons, as a sight.... *Tel 0171/836–5314. 35 Maiden Lane WC2, Covent Garden tube stop. Reservations recommended. Jacket and tie recommended. DC not accepted. £££*

Savoy Grill. The most obvious power lunch in town is staged every weekday, starring newspaper editors, City guys, tycoons, and big shots. Beef Wellington appears on Tuesday; omelette Arnold Bennet (with cheese and smoked fish) was invented here for that novelist. Service is avuncular and discreet; everyone has his (sic) own teal-upholstered banquette on the yew-paneled perimeter; nobodies are plonked in the center, looking at them. It's gentle and touristy by night.... *Tel 0171/836–4343. Strand WC2, Aldwych tube* *stop. Reservations recommended. Jacket and tie required; no jeans. £££££*

Simpsons-in-the-Strand. The Grand Divan Tavern, to give it its full title, prides itself on not having changed—from the heaviest of oak paneling downstairs and Edwardian glitz on the second floor to the roasted animals circulating on silver trolleys, ready to be carved onto your plate. It's like eating on the set of a Merchant-Ivory movie.... *Tel 0171/836–9112. 100 Strand WC2, Aldwych tube stop. Reservations recommended. Jacket and tie required; no jeans. £££*

Soho Soho. The useful parts of this successful trilevel operation are the bar and the rotisserie, where an unpretentious lineup of bistro food (char-grilled chicken, omelettes, calf's liver, fruit tarts) takes second place to the hubbub and hanging out. Plate-glass doors open and spill people onto the sidewalk in summer, and inside is Provençal-tiled. Don't bother with the dull and overpriced second-floor restaurant.... *Tel 0171/494–3491. 11–13 Frith St. W1, Leicester Square tube stop. Reservations not accepted (rotisserie). ££ (rotisserie), £££ (restaurant)*

Star of India. Exuberant owner Reza Mahammad had this once-ordinary high-street Indian restaurant frescoed all over like a Palladian villa, installed star chef Vineet Bhatia and a grand piano on the second floor, and had a hit. Unless you're familiar with the standard canon, you may not realize how different are dishes like *multani bateyr* (boned quail stuffed with chicken and dried fruits and silver-leafed); rabbit, pheasant, or crab tandoori; and *malai khumb khazana* (mushrooms and spinach, in cashew nutmeg sauce). Make sure you go upstairs, and dig that French songstress.... *Tel 0171/373– 2901. 154 Old Brompton Rd. SW5, Gloucester Road tube stop. Reservations recommended. £££*

St. John. The hippest place as soon as it opened, there's no reason why this amusingly spartan refectory should ever lose favor. It's perfectly London. *Guardian* journalists and architects (suits, Arran sweaters, Emporio Armani) devour Fergus Henderson's in-your-face food (salted duck breast and red cabbage; deep-fried lamb's brains; smoked haddock and fennel; treacle tart) and get noisily pissed on French wine. A motto on the menu calls this "nose to tail eating".... *Tel*

0171/251–0848. 26 St. John St. EC1, Farringdon tube stop. Reservations recommended. ££–£££

La Tante Claire. Out of all London's famous chefs, Pierre Koffman is probably the most dedicated to his art; he's certainly the least publicity-courting, and is nearly always at his stove here in Chelsea, which can't necessarily be said for, say, Marco Pierre White. If you're serious about food, and wish to put your money where your mouth is, this is the place to choose.... *Tel 0171/352–6045. 68 Royal Hospital Rd. SW3, Sloane Square tube stop. Reservations recommended. Jacket and tie required. £££££*

Vingt-Quatre. Far in Fulham is this place that claims to be the first genuine *vingt-quatre*-hour, *trois-cent-soixante-cinq*-day restaurant in *Londres*. Details were sparse at press time, but its pedigree is sound—it's the chocolate family's nightlife-entrepreneur son, Joel Cadbury, who owns the place.... *Tel 0171/376–7224. 325 Fulham Road. SW10, Fulham Broadway tube stop.*

Vong. Jean Georges Vongerichten's Manhatten transfer had his attention for its London inception, and fans of the New York branch will recognize many of his Thai-Alsatian hybrid dishes—the charred lamb salad; the lobster-daikon roll with rosemary-ginger dip; the grilled beef and noodles in ginger broth—but it's not New York. It's a tony hotel adjunct, with bootlicking service, glamour styling, and look-at-me, ME, ME! ambiance.... *Tel 0171/235–1010. Berkeley Hotel, Wilton Place SW1, Knightsbridge tube stop. ££££*

Wagamama. Japanese ramen and other noodly/soupy fare, along with "health dishes," and sake and beer are dished out in vast quantity at high speed, and with the aid of high-tech handheld computer order pads at this screamingly successful Bloomsbury eating center. There's always a line for the shared tables, but a fast-moving one. The newer one (tel 0171/292–0990; 10a Lexington St. W1, Piccadilly Circus tube stop) will also give you dessert.... *Tel 0171/ 323–9223. 4 Streatham St. WC1, Tottenham Court Road tube stop. Reservations not accepted. No credit cards. £*

Waxy O'Connor's. "Let's have an Irish pub," said the Beach Blanket Babylon people, "and let's model it on the Book of

Kells and have a Church Room with confessionals, and then let's put a 250-year-old tree and some Dublin houses in the middle, and then let's name it after a drunken Dublin candlemaker." And they built it, and people came. Planet Kilkenny serves a decent pint of Beamish and "crock of mussels" with soda bread, and you can pay in punts.... *Tel 0171/ 287–0255. 16 Rupert St. W1, Leicester square tube stop. Reservations not accepted. DC not accepted. £*

The Westbourne. Not so much rivaling as complementing The Cow, which you can see from the tables out front, this groovers' pub conversion by a couple of art-boys-around-town who know *everyone* is a raging success, from its hardwood floors to its chalkboard of Mediterranean specials. Schmoozing for boozers with design careers.... *Tel 0171/ 221–1332. 101 Westbourne Park Villas W2, Royal Oak tube stop. Reservations not accepted. £–££*

Windsor Castle. A cozy Kensington pub, with a pretty walled garden for summer; open fires for winter; and food from bar snacks of cold British bangers, hard boiled eggs and oysters to pastas, salads, Sunday roasts and steak and kidney pudding.... *Tel 0171/727–8491. 114 Campden Hill Rd. W8, Notting Hill Gare tube stop. Reservations not accepted. £–££*

Wódka. Frequented—heavily—by *beau monde* types who think this is their secret, but actually heard of by anyone who knows London, this minimalist-looking, but warm-feeling restaurant has founded a new genre: modern Polish. Blinis are daubed with eggplant-olive mousse or Osietra caviar; *pierogi* (like ravioli) are fancily stuffed with veal and wild mushrooms.... *Tel 0171/937–6513. 12 St. Alban's Grove W8, Gloucester Road tube stop. Reservations recommended. ££££*

LONDON ☽ LATE NIGHT DINING

down
and
dirty

Babysitters... Ask whether your hotel has a preferred local service. Otherwise, the **Nanny Service** (tel 0171/935–3515; 9 Paddington St. W1) and **Universal Aunts** (tel 0171/738–8937; 19 The Chase SW4) are tried and trusted.

Buses... Those red double-deckers, synonymous with London, are the cheapest tourist attraction in town, plus they get you where you want to go, slo-o-wly. At night, the bus frequency may be down to one per hour. Still, at least the buses keep going all night, unlike the tubes. By no means are all buses double-deckers, but all are hailed the same way—by waiting at the concrete post with flag-like sign on top. By day, if the sign is red, it's a "request stop," and you stick out your arm; otherwise the bus stops automatically (unless there's no room on it). By night, buses behave as if every stop were a "request," so always hail the driver. You can tell you're into night territory by the "N" prefix on the bus number, and you can tell where the bus is going by reading the oblong sign at eye level on the bus stop, but also check the destination sign in front of the bus, since many fail to run the whole route. Daytime fares are assessed on the same system as for the tube, and Travelcards are valid for both modes of transportation (see "Tubes," below). Show your card or pay your coins to the conductor—who often doubles as the driver. For everything longer-lasting than a One Day Travelcard, you'll need a **Photocard**, available free from tube stations—bring a passport-size photo. You can also pick up free bus maps from main tube stations (if you can't find them, call 0171/371–0247). Night buses also accept Travelcards, but *not* the one-day ones. After 10pm, no child fares are available on any bus. Night buses (with the "N" prefix) are all of the pay-as-you-enter type, so have your fare—about double daytime fares—or pass ready. Ask for the free Night Bus Guide when you get your maps.

Car rental... We strongly advise you not to drive in London. You have to do it on the left, use a stick shift, and park. You'll get lost and stuck in one-way systems constantly, and parking is hell, thanks to the usual meters and restrictions. There's also the dreaded "Denver Boot," or wheel clamp—an immobilizing device administered by assiduous independent operators that costs about £120 to get removed. Nighttime parking is never easier, and often even more challenging than by day, and drunk driving is really a stupid idea and very likely to get punished, since the Metropolitan police always have an eye out for funny driving techniques.

If you must rent a car, though, your own driver's licence is all you'll need (though you could also get an International Driver's Permit from AAA). You'll find **Alamo** (tel 800/327-9633), **Avis** (tel 800/331–1212), **Budget** (tel 800/527–0700), and **Hertz** (tel 800/654–3131) in London, charging somewhat higher rates than you may be used to, with unlimited mileage at around £60–80 per day for a mid-size, plus tax, insurance, and extras like a collision damage waiver.

Chauffeurs... When you get that billionaire feeling, step in an **Autofleet** (tel 0181/941–5288) Rolls-Royce, Jag, or Mercedes, or a **Camelot** (tel 0171/235–0234) car with air-conditioning and phone; both from about £100 for 3 hours. Customized tours are given by cabbies with The Knowledge at **Black Taxi Tours of London** (tel 0171/224–2833).

Concessions (discounts)... These are usually available to senior citizens, students, children, and those collecting social security or unemployment benefits at theaters, museums, concerts, and other attractions. Seniors should bring proof of age, and students should never travel without their International Student Identity Card.

Dentists... Round-the-clock emergency dental saviors: tel 0181/677–8383.

Doctors... Doctors on call 24 hours: tel 0181/900–1000. Central London hospitals with 24-hour emergency rooms are: **Charing Cross** (tel 0181/846–1234; Fulham Palace Rd., Hammersmith W6), **Guys** (tel 0171/407–7600; St. Thomas St. SE1), and **St. Thomas's** (tel 0171/928–9292; Lambeth Palace Rd.. SE1), plus the North London **Royal Free** (tel 0171/794–0500; Pond St., Hampstead NW3).

Emergencies... Dial 999 (it's a free call) from any phone for police, fire department, or ambulance.

Events hotline... Dial 01839/123400* for what's on in London this week.

Festivals and special events...

January: The **London International Boat Show** brings the ocean indoors to the biggest exhibition center in town, Earls Court (advance tickets, tel 01733/890–187; box office, tel 01784/473–377; Warwick Rd., Warwick SW5).

February–March: **London Arts Season** packages the arts, with bargain-priced tickets and special events (tel 0171/839–6181; British Travel Centre, 12 Regent St. SW1; phone number works during Arts Season only).

March: **Camden Jazz Festival**, for 10 days in North London (tel 0171/860–5866).

April: The many tiny independent galleries of Notting Hill (around the Portobello and Goldborne roads) that add up to a SoHo NYC–like scene unite for one night, with mass openings.

May: **Chelsea Flower Show** (tel 0171/420–0200; Chelsea Royal Hospital SW3).

June: **Fleadh** (tel 0181/963–0940). Finsbury Park's Celtic music festival is pronounced "flah," and will probably feature Van Morrison, Sinead O'Connor, and whichever Pogues have still got functioning livers. **Spitalfields Music Festival** (tel 0171/377–0287), East London; many concerts are in Hawkesmoor's Christ Church. Season starts at: **Kenwood**; **Holland Park** and **Regent's Park Open Air Theatres** (for info, call 0171/486–2431).

June–July: **LIFT** (London International Festival of Theatre); tel 0171/490–3964. **Wimbledon Lawn Tennis Championships** (tel 0181/946–2244); Church Road, Wimbledon SW19 5AE.

August: **Notting Hill Carnival**, Portobello Road, Ladbroke Grove, All Saints Road Bank Holiday weekend—the big Caribbean extravaganza. Massed camps of North Kensington parade while vast sound systems, goat curry, and gallons of Red Strype amuse the crowds.

July–September: **Henry Wood Promenade Concerts** (the Proms; tel 0171/589–8212; Royal Albert Hall, Kensington Gore SW7 2AP).

November: **Guy Fawkes Day** on the 5th. The day when the lack of success of a 1605 attempt to blow up the Houses of Parliament is commemorated with fireworks and bonfires on which effigies of Mr. Fawkes are incinerated. Check the *Evening Standard* for details of firework displays.

December: **Christmas tree** in Trafalgar Square; many carol-singing sessions, lighting ceremony (London Tourist Board Christmas service, tel 01839/123418*).

Gay and lesbian hotlines... The London Lesbian and Gay Switchboard has 24-hour info and advice at 0171/837–7324. **London Lesbian Line** (tel 0171/251–6911; Tue–Thur 7–10pm, Mon and Fri 2–10pm).

Leaflets and flyers... The rack of leaflets in most museum and many hotel, movie theater, and theater lobbies has information on museums, theaters, and tour operators. The "West End Theatre Guide" is a useful one, and the major national arts organizations—the South Bank

Centre, the Tate Gallery, the Barbican, etc.—also print monthly "what's on" guides. Some of these you can only get from the place itself. A contrasting breed of flyer is the kind advertizing clubs and gigs. If you're at a groovy event, and looking good, you'll get handed a better class of flyer than you'd pick up from shelves in clothing and record stores, bars and venues. Typically, a flyer gives you a reduced cover charge, or lets you in free before 10pm.

Magazines and books... The most useful weekly magazine is *Time Out,* which has easy-to-use listings, plus articles giving background info on the arts, sports, and entertainment events around town. If you're into music, take the weekly tabloid-size *NME* for band background, the monthly *MixMag* for insight into the DJ/clubbing scene, and *Straight No Chaser* for the heppest take on jazz. Gay visitors can get background from the monthly *Gay Times* and listings from the weekly *MX* and *Time Out*'s gay section. If you're going to eat out a lot, invest around £8 in the *Time Out Guide to Eating and Drinking in London*—a comprehensive and reliable guide available from newsagents. Your first purchase at the newsagent, however, should be an *A to Z* (that's "A to *Zed*"), the street atlas that no Londoner is without.

Minicabs... Unlicenced taxis, which can't be hailed on the street, but must be booked by phone or in person at the office. Most hotels and restaurants keep numbers of local services, and will call one for you. Fares are about 25% lower than for black cabs.

Newspapers... London drowns in newsprint. The daily broadsheets, or "qualities," are: the *Times,* the *Guardian, The Independent, The Daily Telegraph,* and the *Financial Times,* while the awful, but entertaining, tabloids are the *Mirror,* the *Mail,* the egregious *Sun,* and the even worse *Star.* Sundays offer a mountain that keeps you occupied all day: the broadsheets *Sunday Times, Observer, Independent on Sunday,* and *Sunday Telegraph,* and the tabs, the *Sunday Mirror, Mail on Sunday,* the *People,* the *News of the World* (a.k.a. "News of the Screws"), and—the father of American *Enquirer*-type mush—the unbelievable *Sunday Sport.* The most useful newspaper for the night owl, however, is the daily evening paper, the *Standard,* out weekdays around lunchtime (especially the Friday edition, for the *ES* magazine with its listings pages).

Pharmacy... Get late-night drugs from **Bliss** (tel 0171/ 723–6116; 5 Marble Arch W1; daily 9am–midnight).

Radio stations... There are five national radio stations: **1FM**, 98.8FM (mainstream pop music, with some indie and alternative music after 10pm); **Radio 2**, 89.1FM (AOR); **Radio 3**, 91.3FM (classical, some talk); **Radio 4**, 93.5FM, 1500m LW (talk, news, game shows, and drama, a beloved national institution, especially "The Archers"—a 30-year-old radio soap about country folk); **Radio 5**, 433m LW (the new one—sports, talk), plus the **World Service**, 463m AM. The principal London stations are: **Capital FM**, 95.8 (pop), **KISS-FM**, 100 (dance/club music), **JFM**, 102.2 (jazz), **Classics FM**, 100.9 (classical), **GLR**, 94.9 (talk, music), **Capital Gold**, 194m AM (oldies), **Virgin**, 247m AM (pop and rock music), and **London News**, 97.3FM. Kiss FM is the one to tune in for clubbing/DJ info, while you can glean more general events information from GLR's talk shows.

Safety... London is still a relatively safe city. Relative to where? Well, according to the past decade's crime figures (published in 1994), it's safer than Los Angeles, New York, and Rio de Janeiro, but more dangerous than Miami, Toronto, and Paris. For instance, London's average annual murder rate in the '80s was one-tenth that of New York's (183:1,859)—which must be largely a result of the fact that personal firearms are not yet an issue in the UK. Still, the usual city precautions for taking care of your property and your person apply. Just use common sense.

Taxis... Hail one when the orange "For Hire" light on the roof is lit. An empty one may stop even if its light is off, since drivers sometimes use this method to screen passengers at night. London cabbies are among the best in the world, since they all have an encyclopedic grasp of London's geography, having passed an exhaustive exam called "The Knowledge." Of this they are justly proud; don't insult your driver by offering directions. Metered fares are £1 for the first 582 yards, rising by 20p per 291 yards or 60 seconds, plus 40p–£2 surcharges for night, holiday, extra passengers or bags, etc.

Theater tickets at half price... The indispensable **Half Price Ticket Booth** (no telephone) on the southwest corner of Leicester Square has tickets for later the same day at about 25 theaters (Mon–Sat 2:30–6:30, from noon for matinees; cash only; £1.50 service charge).

Theater tickets from home... The New York Office of **Keith Prowse** (tel 212/398–1430 or 800/669–8687), or **Edwards & Edwards** (tel 212/944–0290, or 800/223–6108) can arrange your London theater dates; and **Ticketmaster** also has a toll-free US number (tel 800/775–2525). If you're planning a theater fest, are a control freak, and want to do it all yourself, send for the *Complete Guide to London's West End Theatres* (£9.95 plus p&p; tel 0171/836–3193; Society of London Theatre, Bedford Chambers, The Piazza, Covent Garden WC2E 8HQ), which has seating plans and booking information for all the West End houses.

Ticket agents... There's nothing wrong with ticket agents like **First Call** (tel 0171/240–7941) or **Ticketmaster** (tel 0171/413–3321), unless you hate to pay the reasonable booking fee. They are especially handy for major rock gigs, or for when you're having a theater orgy and want to book several shows.

Ticket returns and house seats... Every single theater keeps at least one row of house seats back till the last possible moment for emergency oversales and unexpected situations, plus a dozen or two returns. Policies on how these are dispensed vary, but be prepared to stand on line, possibly in the morning, probably an hour before curtain, with no guarantee of success. On the other hand, you may find yourself in the stalls (orchestra) at the Royal Opera House for a song (i.e., a £85+ seat for about £22).

Ticket scalpers... The big West End musicals, gigs in big places by big names, and major sporting events all harbor a crop of scalpers outside—known as "ticket touts" here. Just say no. Never buy from a guy furtively brandishing a fistful of tickets—common sense will tell you when there's someone with a legitimate extra one. If you get scalped for a West End show, tell your sob story to: tel 0171/836–3193; The Development Officer, Society of London Theatres, Bedford Chambers, The Piazza, Covent Garden WC2E 8HQ. You won't get your money back, but you'll help save future victims.

Tickets... The best place to get tickets for theater, concerts of all genres, and sporting events is directly from the box office, either in person or by phone, with your plastic in hand. See our listings, or look up the number in *Time Out*. (See also "Ticket Agents," above.)

Tickets from classified ads... Ads are often placed in the *Standard* by sort-of-legitimate scalpers who bought blocks of tickets to major sports events, rock shows, and Three Tenors–type extravaganzas, and are off-loading them at a premium. If it's the last minute, this may be your only hope for catching, say, the FA Cup Final (the UK soccer Superbowl), or the Men's Singles Final, Wimbledon.

Tickets from hotel concierges... Hotels—including those with a dedicated theater desk—charge a bigger fee than the phone bookers, and are only worth using if you're lazy, loaded, or longing to see Lloyd Webber's latest, in which case the best of them (the Savoy, the Athenaeum, the Dorchester) may come up with the impossible, pricey ticket.

Travel hotlines... For round-the-clock information on bus and tube times, routes, fares, etc., call 0171/222–1234. For updates on how services are running, call London Travel Check: 0171/222–1200.

Travelers with disabilities... Hot lines include the **Artsline** (tel 0171/388–2227) for advice on accessibility of arts events, and the **Holiday Care Service** (tel 0129/ 377–4535) for help with accommodation questions. London Transport has a **Unit for Disabled Passengers** (tel 0171/222–5600), which includes the Stationlink service, a wheelchair-accessible "midibus" between nine BritRail stations and Victoria Coach Station. **RADAR** (the Royal Association for Disability and Rehabilitation), (tel 0171/250–3222; 12 City Forum, 250 City Rd., London EC14 8AF) publishes travel information for the disabled in Britain.

Tubes... The London subway is the fastest way to get around—usually. There are 11 lines, plus the Docklands Light Railway and the future Metro Express (Haringey to Wimbledon via Soho and Fulham), which may be on maps already, in pale green. They all run Mon–Sat 5am–12:30am, Sun 7am–11:30pm (approximately), and average waiting time is 5 to 10 minutes. Tube fares are assessed in zones, with the price rising according to how many of the six you pass through. The most expensive way to travel is by single ticket (£1–3.10). It's a far better idea to get a **Travelcard** (from £2.80/day, children £1.50), valid all day from 9:30am for tube and bus, or an **LT Card** (valid all hours; from £3.90/day, children £1.90), without time restrictions. For Weekly and Monthly Travelcards, you need a **Photocard** (free at tube stations), as you do for a **Visitor's Travelcard**, which you get in the US from BritRail Travel International (tel 212/382–3737; 1500

Broadway, New York, NY 10036). These come for 3, 4, or 7 days for $25, $32, or $49 ($11, $13, or $21 for children), which includes discount vouchers to London sights. Leaflets explaining ticket types and fare zones, plus tube maps, are all available free from tube-station ticket windows. Warning: You can be fined on the spot for traveling without a valid ticket.

Visitor information... Before you leave home, contact a branch of the **British Tourist Authority** (tel 212/986–2200 or 800/462–2748, 551 Fifth Ave., Suite 701, New York, NY 10176; tel 312/787–0490, Suite 1510, 625 N. Michigan Ave., Chicago, IL 60611; tel 213/628–3525, World Trade Center, 350 S. Figueroa St., Suite 450, Los Angeles, CA 90071; tel 404/432–9635, 2580 Cumberland Pkwy., Suite 470, Atlanta, GA 30339; tel 416/925–6326, 111 Avenue Rd., 4th Floor, Toronto, Ontario M5R 3J8). When you get to London, the main **Tourist Information Centre** is at Victoria Station Forecourt, Mon–Sat 8am–7pm, Sun 8–5; there are others at Heathrow (Terminals 1, 2, and 3), Harrods, and Selfridges, all open to personal callers only. For phone information, you have to pay the premium rate (49p/min. or 39p/min. cheap rate) for the LTB's **Visitorcall** phone guide. Get the menu at 01839/12–3456.*

Walking around... London is usually accused of being a good walking city, but you must add a coda to that: It's great to walk from, say, St. James's up Bond Street and across Regent Street to Soho, but it's an all-night hike to go on foot from Chelsea to Regent's Park. It's very big here. Also, it's damp. However, walking is the best way to see the detail that make London a fun city; cutting through back alleys to find secret courtyards, spying on people's décor at sundown before they've drawn the shades, exploring cobblestoned mews and spotting architectural follies. Most of London is deserted after midnight, which will make walking eerie and scary, or exhilarating, depending on your temperament. It isn't especially dangerous, with the exception of certain parts of Brixton or King's Cross, but see "Safety," above.

* All calls with the 01839 prefix are charged at the premium rate of 39p/min; 49p/min during peak time.